A Christian View of Being and Knowing

A Christian View
of Being and Knowing

AN INTRODUCTION TO PHILOSOPHY

by

JAMES OLIVER BUSWELL, JR.

ZONDERVAN PUBLISHING HOUSE
GRAND RAPIDS   MICHIGAN

Printed in the United States of America

CONTENTS

INTRODUCTION 7

PART I — What Is Philosophy?

    Chapter I. The Definitions 15

    Chapter II. The Categories 33

PART II — Ontology, the Theory of Being

    Chapter III. Materialism 69

    Chapter IV. Idealism 98

    Chapter V. Dualistic Realism 126

Part III — Epistemology, the Theory of Knowing

    Chapter   VI. Between Ontology and Epistemology.163

    Chapter VII. A Priori Theories of Epistemology...168

    Chapter VIII. Constructive Suggestions 178

CONCLUSION 199

EPILOGUE 200

SUGGESTED ASSIGNMENTS 201

BIBLIOGRAPHY 205

INDEX 209

A Christian View of Being and Knowing

INTRODUCTION

A beginning is somewhere. Our physical birth had a location in geography and in history. Dr. Paul A. Sipple, speaking of the difficulty of precisely locating the South Pole, says, "Unless you know exactly where something is on the planet — and the somethings we start with are the poles — it is impossible to determine exactly where anything else is."[1] So every experience, every course of study, every process of inquiry must begin somewhere, sometime, in a location related physically and intellectually to previously existing reality. This textbook, which introduces the student to the general field of philosophy, is not exceptional in that it is written from a particular point of view; though it is somewhat unusual in that the point of view is frankly stated.

There is a dilettante method in the teaching of philosophy which avoids any commitment to convictions other than the conviction that a philosopher should have no convictions. There is even an extreme form of this dilettantism which holds it to be the function of an introductory course in philosophy to unsettle such convictions as the student may have achieved. Such is not the method or the attitude of this book.

It is assumed that the college or seminary students who make use of this text do not come to it with empty heads, or with total lack of orientation to reality. It will be assumed that the student has observed and accepted as his own many good and useful philosophical concepts, though some may be surprised to learn that they already have a philosophy of a sort. Many opinions will need to be changed or redirected. Many convictions will need to be strengthened and viewed in wider relationships. Sometimes the student's assumptions will be rudely shaken, but just as likely, his presuppositions

[1]Dr. Paul A. Sipple, "We Are Living at the South Pole," *National Geographic Magazine,* July, 1957, pp. 26 ff.

will find a deeper foundation and a broader integration. Particularly will this latter be true if the student is an intelligent Christian, for this is frankly a Christian book, and sets forth a Christian view of philosophy.

Our philosophical presuppositions are the basic concepts of the Judeo-Christian tradition. They involve distinctive views, especially in *metaphysics, epistemology* and *ethics,* though all branches of philosophy are more or less colored by these presuppositions.

In *metaphysics* we believe that God is the supreme personal Intelligence, Creator of the finite universe. We hold that the created universe exists, not independently, or as something unrelated or apart; but it is a distinct thing, not part of, or an emanation of, or a thought or act of, but numerically other than its Creator or His thoughts or acts.

We find that the concept of a personal God is complex. The subject-object relationship seems to be essential to personal existence. The Judeo-Christian philosophy does not postulate God as a simple Subject with no object before the universe was created. In the historically manifested Trinity, we find the subject-object relationship existing in God entirely independently of, and prior to, the created universe. Thus the doctrine of finite, temporal creation does not imply discontinuity in God's character, as though objectivity were something new for God. The doctrine is entirely consistent with God's eternal triune existence.

We find in the created universe an important difference between beings which think, and beings which are spatially extended, or spiritual beings and material beings. This is Descartes' distinction between *res cogitans* and *res extensa.* In the body and mind of man we see integrated interaction between the spiritual thinking being, and the material extended being. Historically this view has sometimes been called dualistic realism.[2]

In *epistemology,* we believe that God, the supreme personal Intelligence, has created us to be in some measure capable of intelligent apprehension of truth. We regard the

[2]"Dualistic Realism" and "Realistic Dualism" are interchangeable terms.

8

basic laws of logic as derived from the character of God's intelligence. We reject the dialectic view of paradoxes, the view that both sides of a contradiction may be true. We believe that the truth coheres and does not contradict itself. We hold that there is some degree of correspondence between our thoughts and the beings, qualities and relationships which exist. We believe it profitable to formulate our ideas of discovered truth in verifiable propositions, and we believe that such propositions may be made more and more accurate and comprehensive by the scientific method, that is, by the assiduous application of careful observation, experimentation, and analytical, discriminating thought.

We believe and accept the Bible as the infallible Word of God, and we are prepared to submit reasonable evidence, open to public investigation, in support of the system of doctrine set forth therein.

Most important are our presuppositions in the field of ethics.[3] We find a calamitous situation existing. We call it the problem of moral evil. There is a basic disharmony in man's spiritual world. Within the individual there is a wide discrepancy between what we feel ought to be, and what is. The same is true in human society. Who would say that man's relations to man are what they ought to be? We find moral evil to be universal throughout the entire human race.

The universality of moral evil leads us to two postulates: (1) There must be some primitive cause of moral evil at the historical source of the race, and (2) a wrong relationship with the Creator of the race must have come about in connection with this primitive cause.

Both of these postulates are illuminated by the fact, sociologically observable, that the human race has a kind of spiritual and moral solidarity. There is a sociological principle of group responsibility, and there is the social fact of the

[3]Instead of including an extended discussion of the field of ethics, it has been thought best to leave this field for separate treatment. It is customary in Christian colleges to offer a full semester's work in "Ethics" as an advanced course. However, it seems necessary to include this summary statement in the introduction for the better understanding of the system of basic presuppositions of this book.

action of representatives involving the group. These phenomena for good or for evil are found everywhere in human society. For example, I am implicated in the Declaration of Independence of 1776. Though I was not there in my numerical identity, yet I was there representatively. Morally and spiritually it was my act through my representatives, and the implications and benefits of it affect me today.

These considerations lead us to state our two postulates in terms of some primitive act of corruption on the part of a primitive representative, or federal head, of the race—some primitive human act in violation of the moral character of God, that is, the corruption of man's original character of godliness, the image of God in man. We find the problem stated in divine revelation in such passages as the Book of Genesis, chapter 3, and the Epistle to the Romans, chapter 5. But if these passages were not given, we should be compelled to postulate the substance of what they say. Universal moral evil can reasonably be interpreted as resulting from an original sin against the character of God.

The philosophy of the Judeo-Christian tradition is unique in that it finds the answer to the problem of evil in the cross of Jesus Christ. It is the cross which constitutes the distinctive feature of Christian ethics. We take the act of crucifying Jesus as a world representative event, on the analogy of the original sin. It was a deed committed by the representatives of the entire human race, typifying and comprehending all our moral corruption. Through those who represented me, I was one who spat in His face, and made the crown of thorns, and drove the spikes into His hands and feet, and mocked and derided Him. When He said, "Father forgive them," He substituted Himself for me. He bore my sin and died in my place the death that I deserved.

The Christian ethic centers in the good news that the Son of God voluntarily bore human sin, and offers both pardon and cleansing to all who will accept Him. The representative principle is found here in its supreme ethical and spiritual implications. This principle may be further illustrated by recent history: — Though I am implicated in the declaration of war, by my representatives, on December 7, 1941, yet (though of course I did not) I could have repudiated my representatives and their action. In that case I should have been sent to a concentration camp. Tojo would have been my representative and Pearl Harbor would have been my deed.

In Christian ethics, the individual acknowledges his implication in the original sin of the race, and recognizes that the act of crucifying Jesus represents the moral evil that is in him. But the individual repudiates the primitive federal head and his act of original sin, and experiences a change of orientation. He specifically accepts the One who bore his sin on the cross as his federal head and representative. Thereafter the death on the cross is his death, and the group to which he belongs, the group with which he is in ethical and spiritual solidarity, is no longer the group represented in the original sin, no longer the group who crucified Jesus, but the group who have accepted Him as their Saviour and Lord.

Christian ethics recognizes that not all humanity will repudiate moral evil and accept the cross, but Christian ethics urges the growth and development of the redeemed humanity by every educational and persuasive means.

We are of course completely committed and devoted to the fundamentals of the Christian faith in no mere academic sense. These fundamentals are what we live by. On the other hand, it remains to state the sense in which these distinctive presuppositions, especially the metaphysical, epistemological, and ethical, are held. These presuppositions as stated here are not held in the sense of propositional infallibility. We distinguish our statements about the truth from the truth itself. We are quite conscious that our human formulations are sure to be found in error in some respects as more light is gained.

Nor are these presuppositions held in the sense that they are supposed to include all the answers. We know full well that more truth is to be discovered (or revealed) than we have ever dreamed of. We who accept this system of philosophy accept these presuppositions in a manner similar to that in which the geophysicists accepted the maps and charts

11

scientifically prepared prior to the elaborate studies of the International Geophysical Year which began in July 1957. The scientists were quite conscious that there were discrepancies in their findings. They were prepared to re-examine anything and everything for greater accuracy. But they all recognized that they were examining the earth in an objective sense, that the facts and their changes, processes and relationships were really there, open to investigation. They did not begin the International Geophysical Year in ignorance. They already knew something about their subject. They knew that the four south poles — the geographic pole, spin pole, geomagnetic pole and magnetic pole[4] — are somewhere in known areas. They knew, too, that the high plateau of the geographic pole would give them extremely low temperatures, as compared with the North Pole. They would not have been in any position to advance the cause of science if they had not had reasonably reliable presuppositions to begin with.

Similarly we believe that our attitude toward philosophy, as we state our presuppositions, is the truly scientific one — the attitude most likely to lead to clearer understanding.

The clearly stated point of view of this book should broaden rather than limit its usefulness as a text for a general introductory course in philosophy. Every effort has been made to present important conflicting views in a fair and objective manner. The field is surveyed in such a way that a competent teacher will find a satisfactory outline, even though his personal views in some respects may be divergent.

[4]The four poles here mentioned are referred to in the article by Dr. Sipple cited above.

PART I

WHAT IS PHILOSOPHY?

Chapter I

THE DEFINITIONS

I. The Meaning of the Most General Terms

A. *Philosophy*

The term philosophy comes from two Greek words, *philia* and *sophia*, which together mean "the love of wisdom." Other particular studies, such as biology, sociology and ethics, for example, investigate limited areas of wisdom; but philosophy investigates wisdom as such, wisdom as a whole.

B. *Ontology, Theory of Being*

Wisdom is bipolar (like the earth with its north pole and its south pole). From the point of view of one pole, wisdom means the things we know. In this sense, wisdom as a whole means the sum total of all that may be known, yet not merely the total as an aggregate, or as a mass of particulars. Wisdom as a whole, viewed from this pole, means the over-all unified total view of what may be known.

Since what may be known is commonly called existence or being, wisdom as a whole, viewed from this first pole, means the general nature of being.[1] Philosophy then investigates the general nature of being, that is, of existence. To put it plainly, philosophy asks, "What is the universe made of?"

The name of the aspect of philosophy just described is ontology. This word comes from the Greek word *on* which means "being" (a form of the participle of the verb which

[1] We are here introducing the word "being" in a simple way in its grammatical sense — that which is. The complicated implications and historical variations of the meaning of being will be taken up in the discussion of the categories and in the chapters on metaphysics. Suffice it to say that in this first chapter the word is not used in the sense in which Thomas Aquinas (1225-1274) used it, nor in the sense of the contemporary existentialists, but in its simple ordinary meaning.

means "to be" or "to exist") and the Greek word *logia*,[2] an account or reckoning. Ontology is the account, reckoning, or investigation, of the general nature of being.

C. *Metaphysics*

There is another term, metaphysics, which is used by American philosophers as the equivalent of ontology. British philosophers, it is true, generally use the term metaphysics as simply another word for philosophy. Indeed metaphysics originally meant nothing but "The Writings Which Come After Physics" in the published works of Aristotle (384-322 B.C.). Thus we have no sound historical basis for either the American or the British usage. For the present, however, we choose to employ the term metaphysics as the equivalent of the term ontology, or that aspect of philosophy which investigates the nature of being.

D. *Epistemology, Theory of Knowledge*

But wisdom has another pole, another aspect. Wisdom may mean, not what we know, but the act or process of knowing. From this viewpoint philosophy studies not the nature of being, but the nature of knowing. Speaking plainly again, philosophy asks, "How do we know anything?"

The technical name for the aspect of philosophy which investigates the nature of knowing is epistemology. The word comes from the Greek *episteme* meaning "science," which in turn comes from the verb *epistamai* which means "to know," or "to understand." Epistemology then has to do with the nature of knowing.

II. UNITY AND PLURALITY

Philosophy includes the concept of unity and the concept of plurality. When, therefore, we say to a friend, "What is your philosophy?" we mean "What is your view of wisdom as a whole?" When we say, "What is your ontology (or metaphysics)?" we mean, "What is your view of the nature of being?" When we say, "What is your epistemology?" we mean,

---

[2]Since this is the uniform meaning of "-ology," the word *logia* will usually be omitted in discussing the derivation of terms.

"What is your view of the nature of knowing?" But this implies a unified complexity.

A. *Objections to Dualism*[3]

All this may seem rather simple, but the complications come thick and fast. I have indicated a dualism in wisdom: first, being or what we know, and second, knowing or how we know. On the contrary there are many prominent philosophers who refuse to distinguish being and knowing in this way. Few, indeed, would deny that there is a difference in meaning between the words "ontology" and "epistemology," but many would reject the implications of this distinction. Away with dualism, they say; being and knowing are the same thing under different names.

B. *Idealists;* C. *Experimentalists;* D. *Materialists*

Idealists generally say that whatever is, is, because it is known by a mind — perhaps the mind of God, perhaps a Universal Mind, or perhaps the human mind. On the other hand, experimentalists (popularly called pragmatists) do not admit the existence of mind as such — mind as that which knows. They also deny being as such — being which is not dependent upon being known. Experimentalists generally say mind is nothing but minding, nothing but the inquiry process. Being is nothing but the same process. Being in general is the minding process of human society in general.

A third group of objectors are the materialists. Where the idealists deny being apart from mind and the experimentalists deny both mind and being apart from the process of minding, the materialists are inclined to deny mind and the processes of mind except as the mental may be merely an aspect of the material. Extreme materialists, such as the behaviorists who accepted J. B. Watson's[4] views in psychology,

[3]There are many dualisms which must be recognized by the student of philosophy. The dualism of being and knowing here referred to is not the same as the metaphysical dualism of "dualistic realism" as the latter term is explained below.

[4]Watson's book, *Behaviorism, an Introduction to Comparative Psychology,* was published in 1914.

either deny consciousness or ignore it. Contemporary materialists like Sydney Hook[5] say that all things mental are related to matter and motion as adjectives and adverbs are related to nouns and verbs. This does not seem any clearer than the older materialistic view, which was that thought is a kind of motion of matter, or that mind and minding are nothing but vibrations in the physical brain. Different kinds of materialists generally agree in rejecting the dualistic distinction between being and knowing which has been brought out above.

We see then that while the idealists say all is mind, the experimentalists say all is process, and the materialists say all is matter, many of them agree in avoiding any sharp distinction between being and knowing.

E. *Monism*

Some of the idealists, instrumentalists and materialists who object to the dualism of being and knowing are monists: that is, they believe that ultimately all is unity and not plurality. Monism does not consist in recognizing ultimate unity in what we know and how we know. Monism consists in denying ultimate plurality or complexity of being.

F. *Pluralism*

Not all who object to the definitions with which this chapter began are monists. On the contrary, objection is made by some philosophers who reject the notion of totality, the notion that being and/or knowing may be regarded as a whole. In meetings of the American Philosophical Association one hears prominent philosophers say, "The notion of the universe as a whole is an unintelligible absurdity." Unified totality is indeed a tremendous and complex thought. It must include not only such ideas as the universe of astronomy and the universe of thought, but the much confused notions of time and space, infinity and finitude and the like. Serious philosophers argue that such thoughts inevitably lead to paradoxes — apparent or real contradictions. Universal integration, they say, is impossible. Some of those who object to the idea of

5See the article, "Are Naturalists Materialists?" by Dewey, Hook and Nagel in the *Journal of Philosophy*, Vol. XLII, pp. 515-530.

philosophy as the study of an integrated unified totality are called pluralists. They believe that all is ultimate plurality without unity. Pluralism does not consist in recognizing ultimate complexity in being and knowing. Pluralism consists in denying ultimate integration.

G. *Dualistic Realism*

From this brief discussion of objections it will appear that the definitions with which this chapter begins are based on the assumption that all wisdom is an integrated total system, and that this system may be viewed from two important aspects; the general over-all view of being, and the general over-all view of knowing. Although as an introductory text, this book seeks to give the student an adequate orientation for the understanding of the most important systems of philosophy, yet as indicated in the Introduction, the book does not lack a definite point of view. The system of philosophy, dualistic realism, to which the author adheres may be designated in a preliminary way as integrated dualism, or dualistic integrationism. It recognizes the ultimate unity of plurality and the ultimate plurality (or complexity) of unity. This system makes bold to investigate universal totality, over-all wholeness. At the same time it separates and distinguishes where distinctions are to be found. For example, in philosophy as a whole it distinguishes *what* we know and *how* we know. In metaphysics it distinguishes beings which are known but do not know, i.e., material things, from beings which both know and are known, i.e., spiritual beings. These distinctions are never found to be instances of total unrelatedness. Neither is the unity found to be an undifferentiated blob. Quite the contrary, the matters distinguished are found to be related and integrated in a wholeness. We revert, then, to our original definition: Philosophy is the pursuit of wisdom as a whole.

III. RELATION TO OTHER STUDIES

A. *General Principles of Classification*

The classification of the sciences and branches of learning is bound to be a debatable matter. There is no clear symmetry about them. Here they overlap, and there one finds wide gaps between them. The following circular diagram is only roughly correct in what it may suggest. Only classes of subjects which involve different philosophical problems are listed. All of these subjects were originally regarded as branches of philosophy in the western cultural tradition. In modern universities metaphysics and epistemology are included in philosophy proper, and aside from these only logic and ethics are fairly sure of their places in the philosophy department.

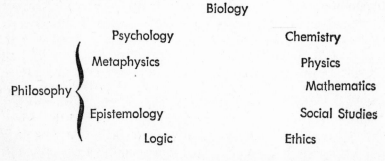

The upper semicircle, with the numerous branches of science which would naturally be classed under those named, indicates sciences in which the nature of being usually receives more attention than the nature of knowing, while in the subjects named in the lower semicircle the nature of knowing generally receives more attention than the nature of being.

B. *Logic*

Moving around the lower semicircle from left to right we find logic to be the subject most closely related to epistemology. The word logic comes from the Greek word *logos* meaning "reason," which comes from *lego* which means "to speak." Aristotle developed his logic from his rhetoric, in his endeavor to teach how to reason correctly as one speaks. Logic pursues the investigation of correct reasoning, reasoning toward the discovery and establishment of truth as distinct from falsehood. Logic is the study of how we *ought* to think if we think correctly.

(1) Normative Science[6]

It is apparent that the definition given here assumes that there is a standard of truth by which the true may be distinguished from the false. A technical word for standard is norm (compare the word "normal," up to "standard"). Logic is therefore called a *normative* science, that is, a study which assumes that there is a norm to which its subject matter ought to conform.

In this sense aesthetics and ethics are also called normative sciences, since they respectively assume standards by which the beautiful may be distinguished from the ugly and the good from the evil. These normative sciences are related to the theory of value. See the discussion of axiology below.

(2) Contrary Opinion

To return to logic, it must be made clear that not everyone agrees that logic is normative. In John Dewey's *Logic* (doubtless his greatest book) he argues strenuously that logic is nothing but the method of the human inquiry process, and that there are no prior laws of logic, there is no permanent standard of truth by which the validity or correctness of the inquiry process may be judged. Philosophical theologians following Albrecht Ritschl (1822-1889) and our contemporaries Karl Barth, Karl Heim, Martin Buber and existentialists and dimensionalists generally, defy the stringencies of logical standards. These influential men advance types of thought which are contrary to the prevailing view from Aristotle down to our own time. The majority of logicians agree that at least the law of contradictories, that is, the principle that truth cannot contradict itself, is a prior standard to which all correct reasoning must conform.

[6]This use of the word "science" is based upon long established custom. See previous discussion of the term "epistemology."

(3) Relation to Epistemology

If epistemology is the theory of knowledge and logic is the science of reasoning, it might be thought that the two would be identical, but this is not the case. Traditional logic must have propositions or formulated statements to begin with. Take, for example, the popular illustration of the deductive syllogism: All men are mortal. Socrates is a man. Therefore, Socrates is mortal. Traditional deductive logic is unable to draw any inference until the first two statements are given. The original statements with which logic must begin are called premises. The reasoning process may be correct whether the premises are true or not, but if the reasoning process is correct, the conclusion is proved to be true only if the premises are true. Inductive logic is likewise dependent upon the truth or falsity of propositions taken as data.

Epistemology goes back of logic and examines the processes by which we may know the data, or the propositions, with which logic begins. Epistemology includes the theory of logical processes, but logic does not include all the basic investigations of epistemology.

(4) Relation to Mathematics

Logic has relationships with all other sciences insofar as they all require valid reasoning. The methods of logic are similar to those of mathematics. This similarity is so obvious as to need no elaboration at this point.

(5) Logic and Psychology

Psychology is commonly compared with logic by saying that the latter investigates how we *ought* to reason, and the former, how we actually think.

(6) Relation to Metaphysics

Many logicians would say that logic is not directly connected with metaphysics. They would say the same about mathematics. The laws of trigonometry hold true regardless of inaccuracy of surveyors' instruments, refraction of light, or errors in calculating. Logic has to do with formal processes of reasoning based upon premises, and the processes are the same whether the premises are true about ontological reality or not. If we assume that all A is B, and all C is A, then all C is also B, whether the terms are real or imaginary, or even absurd.

(7) Law of Sufficient Reason

However, there are rationalistic idealists who hold that *ratio est causa essendi* (reason is the cause of being). For example, D. S. Robinson,[7] following Leibnitz (1646-1716), argues for a "law of sufficient reason." Robinson refers to Josiah Royce (1855-1916), a noted Harvard idealist, as believing in "the logico-mathematical structure of the whole existing universe." Many rationalistic idealists hold to this law of sufficient reason, teaching that everything which exists is what it is, and as it is, because reason (logic and/or mathematics) makes it so.

However, there are many instances in which it is impossible to trace any casual connection between existing being and logic or mathematics. The path of a ray of light through vast astronomical distances does not quite correspond to a straight line in Euclidean geometry. There is probably nothing in the laws or processes of logic, and probably no logical implication, which causes or gives a reason why the largest land masses on earth are in the northern hemisphere, or why the north pole is in an ocean and the south pole in a high continental plateau. In the Judeo-Christian tradition, the grace of God is held to be independent of logical necessity, otherwise grace would not be gratuitous. Although the truth never contradicts itself, and never is *ir*rational, there are many truths about existing things which are *non*-rational, that is, not caused by reason.

(8) Logic and Aesthetics and Ethics

Apart from the fact that aesthetics and ethics both involve valid reasoning processes in the consideration of their data, it might seem that they have little to do with logic. However, there is a popular use of the word "logic" which makes it practically equivalent to the word "appropriateness." For example, in the sentences, "The logic of the situation demanded

[7]*Principles of Reasoning*, third edition, Appleton-Century, 1947, pp. 365 ff.

an explanation from the chairman"; "Navigators in the days of Magellan and Drake logically expected to find great continents in the southern hemisphere"; and "Punishment is the logical result of crime"; we have a use of the word logic which has less to do with valid reasoning processes than with aesthetic feeling or ethical conviction. It is like the dynamic sense of tension toward wholeness brought out in *Gestalt* psychology, like the feeling we have when someone plays the scale up to the seventh and stops. "Logically" we finish the scale with the octave. Probably the best opinion is that this use of the word logic is anomalous and has little to do with the science of logic as such.

C. *Aesthetics and Other Subjects*

The Greek background of the word "aesthetics" implies perception by the senses. The word was used in the eighteenth century to designate perception of beauty, in comparison with logic in which truth is the subject matter. Immanuel Kant (1724-1804) objected to the notion that aesthetics is primarily concerned with beauty, and used the term in a more inclusive sense as signifying the abstract principles of sense perception. However, since Hegel (1770-1831), aesthetics is generally accepted as designating the science of beauty. Aesthetics is obviously related to the fine arts, music, painting, sculpture, architecture and poetry.

(1) Aesthetics and Philosophy

Aesthetics is generally regarded as a branch of philosophy, though seldom taught as a particular subject in the philosophy curriculum. Aesthetics is a part of metaphysics if one believes that beauty is an ontological aspect of existing things. It is a part of epistemology if beauty is thought to be an aspect of knowing. There are those who hold that beauty is merely a matter of feeling, and that it is neither a part of existing things nor a part of the knowing process. Dualistic realism recognizes aesthetics as an aspect of each, metaphysics and epistemology, and holds that beauty involves a special relationship between minds and the things of which minds are conscious. What kind of special relationship beauty involves, or why our minds perceive some things as beautiful and others as ugly, must be investigated further. For the present it will be sufficient to say that as involving a theory of beauty, aesthetics is definitely a part of philosophy.

(2) Aesthetics and Christian Presuppositions

The saying, "Worship the Lord in the beauty of holiness," and similar expressions frequently found in the Bible, indicate a relationship between aesthetics and Christian presuppositions, but Isaiah's description of the coming "Servant of the Lord" shows that mere beauty is not to be taken as an ethical criterion. Isaiah said, "When we shall see him, there is no beauty that we should desire him."

D. *Ethics and Other Subjects*

(1) Ethics and Philosophy

The investigation of the right and the good, and of the problem of moral evil is almost universally regarded as an important branch of philosophy. The relationships between ethics and metaphysics and between ethics and epistemology are extremely complex, depending on the view one takes of the nature of ethics. In the Judeo-Christian tradition the good is an expression of the character of God in relation to personal beings, and evil is any violation of that character as thus expressed. Obviously from this point of view ethics is an aspect of metaphysics, involving the good character of God, and it is also an aspect of epistemology, involving some knowledge of the expression of the character of God.

Among non-theistic philosophers the nature of the good is still regarded by many as a question of the nature of being and knowing. But there are some who hold that good and evil mean nothing but the customary and that which violates custom. Ethics thus becomes for them a mere question of social etiquette, not an important part of philosophy as here defined.

(2) Ethics and Other Sciences

Ethical philosophy is involved in all personal relationships, and so in all branches of human science, especially the social studies.

(3) Ethics and Axiology

It has been noted above that logic, aesthetics and ethics may be called normative sciences, since, at least in the minds of many, they assume norms or standards or criteria in their respective fields of truth, beauty and goodness. A broader term than normative is axiological, from the Greek word *axia* meaning "worth" or "value." Some philosophers who resist the notion of permanent standards are willing to recognize at least that there are values in human experience. Some extremists would reduce all truth value, beauty value and moral value to nothing but pleasure value and would emphasize the unstable relativity of pleasure. Nevertheless it may be urged that there is value in recognizing that there are values, and that values are experienced. The metaphysical and epistemological aspect of the study of values is important. Axiology would seem to extend through the philosophical normative sciences and into the field of social studies.

E. *Social Studies and Philosophy*

Philosophers have always considered it their prerogative to discuss problems of human society. Perhaps in some cases it is an unconscious psychological defense mechanism against the charge that philosophers live in a remote ivory tower far from practical matters. There are too many instances of philosophers making dramatic pronouncements on problems of politics, sociology and especially economics, without adequate knowledge of such solid ground as has been covered by specialists in these fields.

On the other hand, one wonders whether some cranks with social axes to grind have not found the name of philosopher a good escape device in avoiding the painstaking, laborious methods required of good workmen in the social sciences. Few people know what a philosopher is really supposed to know and do!

Nevertheless, philosophy is properly and directly related to the social studies. The writings of Plato (427-347 B.C.) have strong political and sociological tendencies, and *Das Kapital* of Marx (1818-1883) was an application of the materialistic dialectic philosophy of Feuerbach (1804-1872). For better or for worse, if philosophy is to investigate being and knowing in general, it is bound to develop generalized notions about the being and knowing of human social affairs.

F. *Psychology and Other Subjects*

(1) Psychology and Metaphysics

Turning now to the upper semicircle in the previous diagram, we find psychology placed next to metaphysics among those sciences in which the nature of being receives more attention than the nature of knowing. This position of psychology is highly controversial. Psychology was usually taught in the philosophy department a generation ago. Now, if it is not an independent department, it is usually found as a subdivision of the education department. With this change of relationship has gone a change in subject matter. Originally psychology was a study of the *psyche,* the soul or mind. Recent textbooks, if they mention the word "soul," do so as though anxious to repudiate the notion. The word "mind" is not generally allowed to designate any distinguishable being as such, but only a peculiar function. In some cases mind is not a function of a being, but *just* a function, minding. In other cases mind is frankly held to be nothing but a function of the physical brain and nervous system.

In the view of dualistic realism, although it may be admitted that the major part of the time and attention of the psychologist is taken up with the investigation of mental functioning, yet it is counted absurd to think of a functioning without a something which functions, a thinking without a thinker. Thus it is held that psychology cannot avoid its historical connection with metaphysics. It was in psychology, in the thinking of Augustine (354-430) and Descartes (1596-1650), that dualistic metaphysics learned to distinguish the non-material thinking thing from the material extended thing. Those who disagree at this point must still admit that it is important for them to show why psychology is *not* involved with ontological beings who think. Psychology cannot successfully avoid or evade its relationship to metaphysics.

(2) Relations with Epistemology and Logic

As related to the theory of knowledge, psychology is not so much concerned with the truth or validity of what we commonly say we know, as epistemology and logic are. Psychology is interested in the knowing process descriptively, as it is observed in animals and men, as it leads toward mental skills and habits and a state of mind called certitude. Epistemology and logic are interested in the knowing process critically, as it leads toward certainty.[8] Certitude is a psychological state of mind, confidence in what we say we know. Certainty is something more than a state of mind, we hope! When we say that we have reached certainty in the knowledge-seeking process, we mean that the certainty remains and is theoretically attainable by other minds even though our individual minds should slip, forget or become deluded. Certitude is illustrated by Paul's words, "I know whom I have believed, and am persuaded . . .," certainty by his saying, ". . . . another gospel . . . is not a gospel . . . though *we* or an angel from heaven preach any other gospel, let him [or us] be anathema."

(3) Relations with Aesthetics and Ethics

Psychology is related to aesthetics and ethics in obvious ways, chiefly because these two subjects involve psychological states of feeling, sensibility and conscience, as well as processes of reasoning.

(4) Relations with Social Studies

Social psychology is an important subject lying between psychology and sociology. Minds behave differently in social groups from the way in which they behave in individual isolation.

(5) Relations with Laboratory Sciences

Experimental psychology is itself a laboratory science. As psychology studies the relations between mental behavior and the physical nervous system and the functions of certain ductless glands, it is almost a branch of physiology. Its connections with chemistry and physics are not as close as the connections with aspects of biology.

[8]This distinction between certitude and certainty is not universally observed, but it is nevertheless a distinction which points to a real difference.

G. "Natural Philosophy"

Biology, chemistry and physics, in the historical development of our western culture, were originally branches of philosophy. The physical world occupied a large part of the attention of the early Greek philosophers. Both physics and biology bulk large in Aristotle's writings. These sciences did not completely separate themselves from the term "natural philosophy" until the latter part of the nineteenth century.

At the present time there are tremendous influences from these sciences reflecting back upon philosophy. Examples of such influences are the theory of organic evolution, the Heisenberg principle of indeterminacy, the second law of thermodynamics, and the cosmic change of hydrogen into helium — influences which, for better or for worse, have profoundly affected philosophical theories of ontology and epistemology. It even seems that some philosophers quickly change their step for whatever tune the scientists may be playing. Seriously though, no philosophy should ignore the solid achievements of science in the study of the nature of the universe. The scientific observation of the structure of things is relevant to both metaphysics (as to the structure) and epistemology (as to the method of observation).

H. Mathematics and Other Subjects

(1) Mathematics and Philosophy

The philosophy of Pythagoras (582-507 B.C.), which greatly influenced Plato, was largely mathematical. Aristotle has much to say about mathematics. Among our contemporaries, Paul Arthur Schilpp, editor of the *Library of Living Philosophers* published by Northwestern University, devotes one volume to Einstein the mathematician. Carnap and the logical positivists[9] are mathematicians almost as much as they are philosophers. They follow the lead of Russell and Whitehead in making logic a kind of mathematics. One might point to many other important historical and contemporary mathematical philosophers or philosophical mathematicians.

Just how mathematics is related to philosophy and how it

[9] See *Logical Positivism*, A. J. Ayer (ed.) 1959, The Free Press, Glencoe, Ill.

should be classified in its relations with other subjects are difficult questions. It is interesting to note that A. L. Kroeber, the noted anthropologist, in classifying the sciences as aspects of human culture,[10] finds it impossible to fit mathematics into his diagrammatic scheme of classification.

The similarity between mathematics and logic has been noted. In the circular chart, mathematics is placed directly opposite philosophy at the ends of the two semicircles, between the very dissimilar subjects, physics and social studies. The implications of this position are, I think, justifiable. Physics employs mathematics more than almost any other science does, and the social studies are a close second, especially in using the mathematics of statistics. Mathematics is like philosophy in that it is related to all of being and all of knowing, but it is much narrower in that it is purely abstract.

(2) Mathematics and Metaphysics

Mathematics is closely, yet only approximately related to the ontological world. It has to do with laws of abstract relationships. If there were no beings to count, the multiplication tables would still be true, for the proposition "two plus two equals four," does not necessarily have anything to do with objects. It is hypothetical. When we have counted six potatoes we have two times three potatoes, but if one of the six potatoes is dropped and rolls down the gutter, it is still true that two times three is six, even though we have only five potatoes left. The relation of mathematics to metaphysics is the same as the relation of logic to metaphysics as discussed above.

(3) Mathematics, Epistemology and Logic

Mathematics differs from epistemology and logic in that it is narrower in its scope. Epistemology and logic may deal with any kind of truth and knowledge, whether qualitative or quantitative. Mathematics deals with the numerico-quantitative only. Mathematics is like logic in that it assumes certain axioms, for example, that numbers or quantities equal to the same number or quantity are equal to each other, or that a

[10]*The Nature of Culture* by A. L. Kroeber, University of Chicago Press, 1952, pp. 66-78, from an article published in 1936.

number or quantity as a whole, that is, a finite totality, is greater than any one of its parts. Epistemology goes behind these axioms to investigate their validity. For example when the mathematicians wandered out of their field and tried to destroy their own axiom of parts and the whole, Aristotle (*Physics,* Book IV, Chap. 11, 220 a, 18-20) the philosopher had to remind them that points are not parts of lines; only lines can be parts of lines. Similarly the modern philosopher has to keep the wandering mathematician in line with his own axioms. The mathematician with unconscionable shifting of meanings of words, sometimes talks as if infinity could be called a "whole." It is the epistemologist who has to remind the mathematician that infinity is never a totality, and to call infinity a "whole" is a screaming contradiction.

Conclusion

In this chapter we have defined a number of terms involved in the study of philosophy and have surveyed the relationships between philosophy and other branches of learning. The positions taken are not new or original, but rather, follow the historical main highway. All of this has been given in the simplest terms. The beginner in philosophy must be warned, however, that every definition given, every relationship pointed out, is highly controversial. Every statement made is disputed by some persons who may be considered competent in philosophy. Only a few of the divergent views have been mentioned. These and others will be discussed more fully in subsequent chapters.

At this point, the student must be urged to begin the diligent use of general and specialized dictionaries and encyclopedias. As long as you live with an active mind, you will be obliged to use reference works so that you may understand and use words correctly. As a friend of mine, a chemist, puts it, "Let the philosophy students begin at once to bear the scholar's burden."

Take the last fly leaf at the end of the book. Write at the top, "My New Vocabulary." Jot down every new word you meet, with a phrase to remind you of its definition. You will probably find this the most valuable page in the book.

I hold, of course, that the statements made in this chapter are true as intended and in their context. I believe that the positions taken are correct and defensible, that the relationships pointed out are both real and important, and that the definitions given are supported by good usage and will be conducive to clarity of thought. However, for the many teachers of philosophy who will more or less disagree, I would state that the purpose of this chapter, and of this book as a whole, is to enable the student to find his way around among the philosophies which he will encounter. However one may disagree, I believe that this chapter is near enough to the center of our philosophical heritage to lead the student toward a mature point of view, from which he may discern such errors, and appreciate such values, as may be discovered in it.

CHAPTER II

THE CATEGORIES

A. *Categories Are Predicates*

One should not try to take many steps in philosophy without a clear idea of his categories. Many philosophers and would-be philosophers have failed to observe this principle and have led themselves and others into great confusion. Suppose someone joyously announces, "Pollyanna can walk!" We might think, "Then they won't need to buy a wheel chair," supposing her to be in the category of living human beings. However, when we find that Pollyanna is a character in fiction, in the category of imaginary beings, we remark "What a happy conclusion to a story!" Was Pollyanna *real?* Of course! Not in the flesh, but in a book; not in physiology, but in imagination. She "really" is a character in fiction.

Perhaps the lugubrious, vague and murky nebulosities of the contemporary movement called existentialism[1] may be charged to a failure, or an unwillingness, to clarify the categories. One finds the existentialists usually quite reluctant to state, or even to think, in what particular category their predications lie.

The word "category" is from a Greek word which means "predicate," in the grammatical sense. When we say that categories are predicates in the grammatical sense we do not mean that the items to be classified are always mentioned in the predicates of sentences. In the illustration given above, "Pollyanna" is actually the subject of the sentence, "Pollyanna can walk." What is meant is that if one should say, "What is

[1]See John Herman Randall's incisive remarks on existentialism, and on analysis philosophies, in an article on "The Future of John Dewey's Philosophy" in *The Journal of Philosophy* for Dec. 17, 1959, Vol. LVI, No. 26. See also John Wild "Existentialism as a Philosophy," *Journal of Philosophy*, Jan. 21, 1960. See especially *Christianity and Existentialism* by J. M. Spier, 1953, Presb. and Ref. Pub. Co.

Pollyanna?" or "Define Pollyanna," the predicate of the definition or the predicate in answer to the question, "What?" must be the category in which Pollyanna is to be found. Thus, when we said, "Pollyanna is a character in fiction," "character in fiction" is the predicate or category to which Pollyanna belongs.

In philosophical usage, the categories are not just particular predicates. They are classes or kinds of predicates, classes or kinds of assertions. Any class or kind of predicate may be called a category, but in philosophy it is customary to designate as categories only those important kinds of predicates, denial of which would involve the denial of a large part of the common experience of mankind. Thus, time and space are almost universally regarded as categories. If one denies that time and space are properly predicated of many things, a large section of common human experience would thereby be denied. The same is true of the categories of cause and effect.

B. *Clarity Rather Than Comprehensiveness*

The importance of categories is not so much in the elaboration of an exhaustive list which will include all possible predication, as in knowing in what categories the things we are talking about belong. One finds ten categories enumerated in Aristotle's *Logic,* but he is not at all consistent in his references to them. In several passages he gives lists which omit some of the ten. It is evident that he did not consider his ten categories a complete or exhaustive list. He regarded them rather as important examples. Probably no philosopher will ever elaborate a complete system of categories or any list of main headings under which all possible assertions could be grouped. Completeness is not important, but it is important that one who makes an assertion should know what kind of assertion he is making. When one says, "This is a point," it is important to know whether he means a sharp material object, or an abstract geometrical concept, or an argument in a speech.

C. *Consistency Rather Than Agreement with Others*

The importance of categories is not so much in correctness or agreement with the categories of other persons, as in consistency. Indeed, correctness is important, as we have already indicated. Agreement with others in categorical distinctions is also important. We create needless confusion if we do not try to speak in the terminology of those to whom we speak. But if a writer has in mind clear-cut meanings, and is consistent in his use of terms referring to various categories, we may understand what he means, even though we may think him incorrect in his classifications, and out of line with accepted usage. For example, the personalists generally deny that the category of non-personal matter is a valid predicate. Yet, rejecting their view, I can read and clearly understand Brightman, Knudson and Bertocci (personalists from Boston University). I could even eat sandwiches with them, though I think they should feel like cannibals — eating refreshments whose essential being is personal! They define their personal category clearly and use the word consistently.

D. *Relation to Ontology, Epistemology and Discourse*

Sometimes we think of the categories as classes of being, or kinds of reality. It is possible to work out a valuable system of categories from the viewpoint of ontology, as Aristotle did. Again we may think of the categories as kinds of knowing, classes of cognitive processes or concepts. It is quite possible to develop a practical system of categories, as Kant tried to do, from the epistemological point of view.

It may well be considered, however, that, in a practical way, all we can say about being and knowing, ontology and epistemology, is found in the predications of discourse. All assertions about what is what, about what things are, all categories, are alleged knowings about alleged beings. All categories of discourse therefore purport to be either ontological or epistemological or both. Moreover, we do not need to know whether the alleged knowings or alleged beings are true knowings or true beings, in order to classify them as categories of discourse. Therefore a system of categories based upon a classification of important kinds of predicates found in human discourse is possible, and practicable, prior to any elaborate development of systems of ontology and epistemology.

This fact abundantly justifies the location of this chapter on the categories before the chapters on the several systems of metaphysics and the several theories of knowledge. It is believed that this order of topics will be of great advantage in clarifying the thinking of the student as he moves forward into the ramifications of philosophy.

The problem before us as we seek to set forth a system of categories is to point out the chief classes of assertions or predications which are found in what people say and write. The problem is descriptive and explanatory, not argumentative. Whether assertions are true or false, wise or absurd, what are the chief kinds of predications which people make?

E. *Substantive Entities*[2]

Perhaps the most common categories of human discourse are the substantive entities. Of these there are two kinds, two sub-categories, extended things and thinking things.

(1) Extended Things

The statements that certain things are a stick of wood, a stone, a building, a planet, an atom, an electric charge, a gravitational field, all relate to space-occupying substantive entities. These are material things generally supposed to be composed of what we call matter and/or force. This is the category which Descartes (1596-1650) designated by the Latin words, *res extensa*. Idealists generally deny the existence of material things, other than in idea, but rightly or wrongly, a large part of human discourse is made up of statements about matter and the fields of force which play upon matter.

(2) Thinking Things

Another sub-class of assertions may be illustrated by the statements, this is a great mind, a genius, a moron, an idiot, a schizophrenic person. All these predications designate alleged knowledge of alleged beings in the category of things

[2]The term "substantive entity" is not in common usage, but it seems more suitable for the purpose, and less ambiguous than any other term I have found.

which think — Descartes' *res cogitans*. Materialists generally hold that it is the physical brain which thinks, and thus they deny thinking things as a distinct category. Experimentalists (pragmatists) who follow Dewey's philosophy vigorously deny that there is any substantive entity which does the thinking. They consider it important that thought goes on, but the notion of a thinker is anathema. Some experimentalists, including Dewey himself, deny both the thinking subject and the material object of thought. Nevertheless, as F. R. Tennant, contemporary British philosopher, has pointed out, human discourse almost universally assumes the so-called knowledge of so-called objects by so-called subjects. Tennant says, "No one ever has really dispensed with the subject of consciousness, whatever terms he may have used to hush up its existence. No one ever will dispense with it, because to do so involves intrinsic impossibility. The subject is a logical substance or substantive, involved in affirming the existence of an experience, whether an experience be described as a state or as a relation. A subjectless experience is not merely an absurdity: a contradiction in meanings, if should be a contradiction in terms. . . . the existence of the subject, as distinct from what appears to it, is incapable of gainsaying."[3] No one can deny that thinking things or minds constitute an important category in discourse.

F. *Extension;* G. *Duration*[4]

It is common experience that both what we call matter and what we call mind are always found in two important relationships. First, there is the relationship of being here or there in different directions, or being in what we call *space*. Then there is the relationship of being before and after in different orders of sequence, the relationship of being in what we call *time*.

(1) Assumptions Concerning Space

In discussing space (and time as well) we make certain assumptions, not because the assumptions are inexplicable nor

---

[3]*Philosophical Theology,* Vol. I, p. 18.

[4]The definitions of time and space given in this chapter should be regarded as what are called "precising" definitions. See Copi's *Introduction to Logic,* chapter on "Definition."

because the matters referred to are indefinable, but because it is believed that almost all human beings will recognize these assumptions as elements in daily experience. We are not indeed assuming our definitions, we are not arguing in a circle. All definitions must assume experiences of some kind or other. For example, in physics and psychology there is much argument as to the nature and definition of light. Light has, in the past, been held to be ether waves. Now it is thought that there is no such thing as ether. Light may be composed of particles, or as Eddington, a contemporary British physicist, says, "wavicles." In any case it is assumed that people have the common experience of seeing light, whatever it may be. The experience alone does not give the definition, but the definition presupposes the experience.

(a) The Experience of Extension

In discussing space, we assume that people generally have the experience of extension. There is indeed a special sense of place relationships in our bodies, the kinesthetic sense, the nerve end organs of which are situated in our muscles, tendons and joints. By this kinesthetic sense we know where our legs and arms are in the dark. In the nerve disease called locomotor ataxia, kinesthesia is destroyed and the patient cannot properly locate his members unless he can see, cannot walk in the dark. The sense of space relationships is not entirely lost in locomotor ataxia however, for the patient can locate his limbs if he can see. He still retains a sense of things being here, there, above, below, in or out.

(b) The Experience of Measurement

It should be noted that the experience of extension is an experience of manifold relativity. Observed objects are extended in an infinite number of directions, and by an infinite number of degrees or distances. From ancient times men have measured extension by comparison of one length with another, a foot, a forearm (cubit), etc. Bridgman,[5] a contemporary Harvard professor, has well pointed out that the concept of length is equivalent to the concept of comparative measurement. This is true whether the distances be astronom-

[5]*The Logic of Modern Physics,* Macmillan, 1946.

ical or sub-microscopic. Not that extension is nothing but comparative measurement, but the *concept* of extension involves the concept of comparison.

Any definite measurement may be called a dimension; but the student should watch for highly specialized usages of the word, both in mathematics and in figurative rhetoric.[6]

(2) Figurative or Derived Meanings

The student should not be deceived by the fact that the words here, there, above, below, etc., are sometimes used in a figurative or derived sense to designate relationships other than those of extension. For example we say, "He is not all *there*"; "He is *absent* minded"; "He is *above* reproach."

Even the very words extension and space are used in a derived or figurative sense. Such expressions as, "having the time extended," "a brief space of time," are not uncommon. We also speak of "this world of time and space," meaning the present world order, as contrasted with a different order called "eternity." These are examples of good usage, but they do not disprove the fact that the literal and primary meaning of the words is abstracted from the common experience of extension.

(3) The Meaning of Space — Not a Substance

We have assumed the common experiences of extension and measurement of extension. It has been made clear that the experience of spatial relationships does not define space any more than the experience of light tells us what light is. We now face the question of the meaning of the category of space — the literal meaning, that is, not the figurative meanings referred to above.

Negatively, then, by the word space we do not mean any substantive entity, material or mental. Space is not any kind of substance. We cannot chop out a section of space and move it. It may seem paradoxical to say that space is not

[6]The assumption of "three dimensional space" is the assumption that not more than three planes, each perpendicular to the others, may meet at any given point. This assumption does not deny the necessity for more than three coordinate dimensions, as in mechanics. Figuratively, the word dimension is used to refer to any given aspect of a situation.

an extended substantive entity. Yet the number ten is not ten counted things. Abstract nouns are not the objects from which they are abstracted. Space is that in which extension occurs, or may occur. We are not discussing the question whether there is any empty space, or whether in what is called a vacuum there may be rare gases, or whether hydrogen atoms are found in all astronomical space. Whatever is or is not in space, is not what we mean when we use the term space, since space is not any kind of substance.

(4) Space Not Boundaries

When we speak of a particular space, we refer to a part of space conceived as having boundaries, physical or imaginary. The boundaries, though they may be in space, are not space itself. They do not cut or confine space itself. They merely define a particular area in space.

(5) Space Not a Container with Boundaries

Space in general does not mean a bounded or limited container. To say that a thing is in space means either that it has extension as one of its attributes (as all material things are said to have), or that, like a geometrical point, or like a human mind, it has a location, or performs actions, with reference to extended things. If we say that God is in space, we do not mean that He is contained in anything, but that He acts in and upon extended things and local things. This is involved in the doctrine of the omnipresence of God. God is not an extended being, partly here and partly there. God is everywhere as a total personal presence.

The very notion of general space as a container is a contradiction, for a container by definition has boundaries, and boundaries by definition have a beyond, extending in dimensions on all sides. To ask about the boundaries of space in general requires one to ask what space is beyond space. So then if space itself were a container, we should have extension outside of space, or space which is not space.

(6) Space Means Room, a Workable Definition

Coming to the affirmative aspect of the definition, we must say that space in human discourse signifies an abstract concept of room. Compare the German word for space, *Raum*. Just as the equation "two plus two equals four" is an abstraction[7] and does not necessarily refer to any existing objects, so the general term space has no necessary reference to any extended objects or locations. Extension is a characteristic of concrete material objects. The idea of space as such is the abstract concept of possible relationships in all directions in extension. Space may be empty or full. Wherever we can think "here and there," there is space. *Space is the mere abstract possibility of dimensional relationships.*

(7) Assumption Concerning Time, the Experience of Duration

Time is not indefinable[8] but every definition in human language must assume some previous knowledge. In discussing the category of time it seems reasonable to assume the common human experience of duration, and sequence of events, the experience of before and after relationships. The experience does not give the definition, but may be assumed as prior to it. If anyone is not willing to assume this common experience, then in dealing with him we shall have to find some other common ground of assumption from which the experience of duration through sequence of events may be analyzed. Except for a quibbler, however, this will probably be unnecessary.

(a) Experience of Duration Relative

The experience of duration, as commonly observed, is a relative matter. There is the perduring experiencer who is able to say that the events in sequence have the quality of somehow belonging to him, and there are the many series of events which are observed to occur one after the other in related and interwoven sequences.

In history men have observed the relative velocity of dif-

[7]The words "abstract" and "abstraction" should be taken in the simplest sense. An abstract term refers to a quality or a relationship apart from the objects to which the quality or relationship may belong. Thus, honesty and height are abstractions; an honest man and a high mountain are concrete beings.
[8]Men may differ in their ability to define their terms, but it is amazing to find a modern philosopher hiding behind "the indefinable." What right has anyone to use a word if he cannot at least tell what he means by it?

ferent series of events, and have measured the velocity of one series of events by that of another. The most common standard of measuring relative velocity is the course of the sun, and as long as we live on this earth we shall probably continue to measure by this standard. Yet we have a sense of time which is philosophically, if not physiologically, comparable to our kinesthetic sense of location. We know our memories, as distinct from present experiences, with some degree of certainty; and we distinguish both from our imagination and from our anticipation of future experiences. Moreover, in instances of rhythm large numbers of persons are capable of keeping almost perfect synchronism, merely by their common sensibility of intervals of duration. The sense of time differs from kinesthesia in that the latter seems to function through specialized nerve organs, while the former seems to function through any or all sensory organs. The sense of time is keener in some individuals than in others, and it is capable of being developed to some extent by training.

(b) Twofold Experience

It is important to note that when we experience duration, our experiences are of two kinds. For one thing we observe events in which objects are involved. Again, however, we experience the before-after relationships of these events. There is nothing very mysterious about observing these before-after relationships. The experience seems to be as direct an intuition as observing the yellow color of a dandelion. It is there whether we like it or not. But when events in which objects are involved have these before-after relationships, we call this *being in time*. This leads us to the question, "What is time?"

(8) Figurative or Derived Use of Terms

As in the case of words referring to spatial relationships, we find that such words as "before," "after," "prior," "subsequent" are used in senses other than those directly related to the common experience of duration. We say "Five comes before six," but this is because we usually count "up" from one. For similar reasons we say, "A comes before B." In the expression "logical priority" we do not directly refer to priority in time. Indirectly, however, the words "before," "after," "prior," "subsequent," are used in other than temporal senses because of the *analogy* of time sequence. The primary meaning of the word time and other related words lies within the experience of duration which is common to human beings.

When Tennyson says,

For though from out the bourne of time and place
The flood may bear me far,
I hope to see my Pilot face to face,
When I have crossed the bar,

it is clear that he is using "time and place" figuratively, designating the present world order by metonymy. Tennyson could not have meant literally that he would get outside of general time and space, for the very words "from," "out," "far," "face to face," "when," "crossed the bar," indicate that he contemplated extension and duration in the "Other World."

(9) Time Not a Flowing Substance

When it comes to a definition of time we find the situation even more complex than in the definition of space. Again we must state the negatives first, eliminating false conceptions. Negatively then, time is not a stream of flowing stuff. It does not flow forward or backward or in any direction. Neither does it stand still while other streams flow. Time is not the sum-total of all flowing processes, nor any one process like the course of the sun. Time is not a substance. Parts of time are not substantive entities which could be moved about.

(10) Time Not a Container

Continuing negatively, time is not a container. When we say that objective beings are *in* time, we mean that they have duration or continuity, along with other beings, while processes of events go on in sequence. In the case of instants in time, which have no duration, but are related to time as points are related to space, we say that instants are in time because they have the before-after relationship to events and beings which have duration. When we say that God is in time we do not mean that God is in a container, any more than when we say that God is in space. We mean that God has duration, and acts in and upon events and objects which have duration. A god who is not in time and space is not eternal. He would be a god who has no duration and does not act in or upon events or objects in time and space. When Jesus said, "Before Abraham was, I am,"[9] He was asserting the eternal duration and the time relatedness of His deity.

A particular time may be thought of as limited or bounded by certain events. Thus, the time of my philosophy class has been from nine-thirty to twelve on Wednesdays. When the clock indicates twelve, time is up for the class, but time in general is not thus limited. To regard time as limited would immediately provoke the question, what is *before* and *after* the limits?

(11) Occasion and Duration

In the Greek language there are two different words for time. *Kairos* means a particular occasion; *chronos* means time in the sense of duration, whether time in general, or the duration of a specified process. John quotes "the Mighty Angel" as saying, "that there should be time [*chronos*] no longer: But in the days of the voice of the seventh angel, when he shall begin to sound [his trumpet] the mystery of God should be finished, as he hath declared to his servants the prophets."[10] It is clear from the context that here there is no reference to the end of time in general. John is speaking of the ending of a specific process, or situation, which he calls "the mystery[11] of God." Time will be up for this "mystery."

(12) Aristotle's Concept of Time

The word time in human discourse, like the word space, indicates an abstraction. Aristotle almost said this in his *Physics*, Book IV, Chapters X and XI. He says, "It is evident then that time is neither movement nor independent of movement . . . when we do perceive a 'before' and an 'after' then we say that there is time. For time is just this, number of motion in respect of 'before' and 'after.' Hence time is not

[9]John 8:58.
[10]Revelation 10:6, 7.
[11]I have suggested elsewhere that this "mystery" is the Church as constituted in the present age. Cf. Ephesians 3:3-6.

movement, but only movement insofar as it admits of enumeration. . . . Time then is a kind of a number. Since number is of two kinds, (1) that which is counted, or the countable, and (2) that with which we count, time is really the thing counted, and not that with which we count. That with which we count is different from that which is counted."

(a) Aristotle's Mistake

The last sentences of this quotation (Aristotle's *Physics,* Book IV, Chapter XI, Section 219 b, lines 1-9) reveal, in my judgment, one of the most unfortunate mistakes in the whole history of philosophy. In an unpublished paper[12] on Thomas Aquinas I have traced the effects of this teaching of Aristotle's in the thought of Augustine and Thomas. The point is that whereas Aristotle saw that time is similar to number, and thus he was within a hair's breadth of saying that the concept of time is an abstraction, he chose instead to say that time is not like the abstraction with which we count, but that time is like the concrete things counted.

Number as *that with which we count* would have given a far better analogy to time. In this usage, when I say, "five," I mean I have an abstract concept of units which may or may not exist, a concept which does not designate any particular objects or units, but which may be applied to any five units. If time were taken as analogous to this meaning of number, time would not mean any actual sequence, but would be a mode of conceiving of any sequence which might occur.

On the other hand when I take number as meaning *that which is counted,* if I say, "five," I must mean something like, "five potatoes." Aristotle does not say "potatoes," but, using "number" as *that which is counted,* he says (Section 220 a, line 24), "Number, e.g., ten, is the number of these horses, and so in other cases." On this analogy time must be conceived as some actual sequence. By making this choice Aristotle understood time to be, not an abstraction, but the actual on-going of events, "[actual] movement insofar as it admits of enumeration."

[12]Multilith copies available from Covenant College Book Store, Route 1, St. Louis 41, Missouri.

(b) The Right to Criticize

But what right have we to criticize a definition if it is consistently adhered to? None whatever. The people of Boston have a perfect right to name a certain street Summer Street up to a certain intersection, and then name the continuation of it Winter Street. However, there are systems of road names which facilitate the arrival of travelers at their destinations. The State of New Jersey has re-numbered some of its highways to greatly simplify directions given to strangers.

(c) Augustine's Dilemma

Aristotle had a perfect right to entangle his definition of time with the actual on-going of the world process, but in so doing he threw Augustine into a dither over the question of time before creation. If time is inextricably involved in actual sequence of cosmic events, there could be no time before the cosmos existed. For those who like Augustine believe in creation in the sense of an absolute beginning of the cosmic process, if time is actual sequence of finite events, there could be no time before creation. But the necessary word "before" in the phrase "before creation" involves the contradictory concept of time before time!

(d) Contradiction Unavoidable

Those who do not believe in an absolute beginning of the cosmic process are not compelled to accept the notion of time before time, but, if they follow Aristotle, they cannot escape the contradiction in thought involved if they accept Aristotle's definition. Physicists tell us that it is possible that the cosmic process may come to a dead end, a stable equilibrium, in which no events will take place, no sequence will continue. Bertrand Russell and the late George Santayana have so taught. After this dead end, on Aristotle's definition, time would be no more, but the word "after" demands time after time has ceased.

Both an absolute beginning and a complete ending of the cosmic process are rational, that is, non-contradictory, concepts. But on Aristotle's definition this means that perfectly rational concepts involve the irrational corollaries of time before the beginning of time, and time after the end of time.

(e) Inconvenient Name

It is as though Aristotle gave the name time to the county loop road which encircles the entire city and comes back to meet itself at a crossing. If he had chosen to say, "Time is like number conceived as the abstraction with which we count," it would have been like giving the name time to Main Street, which runs straight through the city and is capable of extension indefinitely as new subdivisions are added.

(13) A Workable Definition

Time therefore should be defined[13] as the *mere abstract possibility of relationships in durational sequence.* The question then, "What would come after the hypothetical end of time?" or the question, "What was before the beginning of time?" would be like the question, "What would happen if the multiplication tables should fail?" or, "What was true before the laws of logic were enacted?" Simply, it is always true that two plus two equals four, that two contradictory propositions cannot both be true, and similarly, it is always abstractly possible that events in durational sequence may occur. When finite units are created, propositions are made, and events occur, then these abstract truths are applied to concrete particulars. It thus appears that the definition of time as an abstraction, *the mere abstract possibility of relationships in durational sequence,* serves as an adequate description of what we mean when we say that beings and events are *in time.*

(14) Paradoxes of Space and Time

Zeno of Elia (a Greek town in southern Italy), who lived in the first part of the fifth century B.C., presented to the philosophical world of his day the paradox of motion in space and time. The paradox was developed under several different illustrations, but the substance of it is that before an object moves from one place to another it must move half as far and before it moves half the distance it must move a quarter of the distance, and so on. Numbers never stop, and fractions can be continued to the infinitesimal. Space is infinitely divisible, so

---

[13]Oscar Cullman, *Christus und die Zeit,* Zurich, 1946. English translation *Christ and Time,* Westminster Press, seems to assume a definition of "time" similar to the definition here given. Eternity is not timelessness.

that there is no limit to the smallness of the infinitesimal parts. Space can be thought of as composed of any given number of infinitesimal parts. But *infinitesimal parts* were confused with points. Now points are *zero* space. Infinity times zero equals zero. Between any two points in space there are an infinite number of points, but these do not constitute or compose any space at all. It is not true that between any two points there are an infinite number of *parts* of space. However small may be the divisions of space between two points, if the part is multiplied by the same number (not infinity) by which the space was divided, the original space is exactly filled. "The part next to a part" of space is an intelligible phrase, but "the point next to a point" is an absurdity. "Next" means contiguous, and if two points are contiguous they are identical.

Confusing *points* with infinitesimal *parts*, it was held that space is composed of *points*, such that between any two *points* there are an infinite number of *parts*, of space. But the point (part) next to the one occupied is infinitely separated by points (parts). Zeno argued therefore that motion in space and time is an illusion.

To my way of thinking Aristotle satisfactorily answered Zeno in Book IV of his *Physics*.[14] Aristotle makes it perfectly plain that *points are not parts of lines*. Only lines are parts of lines; points are not parts of space; only spaces are parts of space; instants are not parts of time. Only durations (moments, not instants) are parts of time. Now since both space and time can be divided into portions as small as anyone desires, for every small or large amount of space in which an object is moving there is a corresponding small or large amount of time. An object does not move in points or instants, but it moves in a state of motion in *portions* of space and time. If the student will remember that *points are not parts of space* and *instants are not parts of time*, he can see through most of the forms of the so-called paradox of motion in space and time.

[14]See particularly chapter XI, section 220 a, lines 18-20.

H. *The Category of Quality*

(1), (2) Definitive and Additive Qualities

In ordinary discourse all substantive entities[15] are assumed to have attributes or qualities by which they may be known. Let us begin the study of the category of quality by suggesting a simple twofold classification: first, definitive qualities, or those qualities which are analyzed from the definition of that of which they are qualities; second, additive qualities, or qualities which may be synthetically[16] predicated of that to which they belong. For illustrations of the first class, definitive or analytic qualities, we may note that extension in space and duration in time are commonly regarded as essential to the definition of all material beings. Having flesh and blood and having some degree of intelligence are also definitive qualities; that is, they are part of what it is to be human. On the other hand lightness or darkness and particular color of eyes and hair are additive or synthetic qualities of man. Having some kind of pitch and having some kind of timbre are definitive qualities of all sounds, but particular pitch and timbre are usually synthetic qualities.

In the majority of cases color is observed as a synthetic attribute. It is not at all important to elaborate a system of definitive and additive qualities, but it is important to realize that some qualities are spoken of as being essential to what it is to be the thing referred to (Aristotle's oft repeated *to ti en einai*), and some qualities as not thus essential.

(3) Qualities Apprehended by the Senses

We have mentioned color and pitch as, in most cases, additive or synthetic qualities. With these may be classed taste, smell and touch (or contact). If we substitute the broader terms sight and sound for the narrower color and

[15]Not only substantive entities, but mental images, acts, relationships, and qualities themselves, have qualities.

[16]For the present discussion the words "definitive," "analytical," and "essential" may be considered as roughly synonymous when applied to the first class of qualities, and the words "additive" and "synthetic" similarly synonymous as to the second class. The noted English philosopher John Locke (1632-1704) designated these two classes as "primary qualities" and "secondary qualities," in their application to material objects. The designation adopted here is applicable to things in all categories.

pitch, we have a list of five attributes of material objects which are apprehended by the most commonly recognized senses. In each case there is assumed a quality of the object independent of the human sense organ — a physico-chemical state or activity or vibration — and in each case there is assumed a relationship of this objective quality to the sense organs, and through the sense organs to consciousness.

(a) Two Conflicting Definitions

Argument has been wasted over the question whether there is color in the rose apart from the eye which sees it, or sound in the waterfall apart from the ear which hears it. It is a question of definition. If color and sound are defined as the physical situations which give occasion to the experiences, then color and sound are to be regarded as independent of experience; but if they are defined as experiences of consciousness, then that is what they are, and there is no color or sound or taste or smell or touch without the sensory experience.

On this second definition, the internal or subjective view, the difference between color experience which we have when we see a rose, and our color experience when we have a dream or hallucination, may be explained by the dualistic realist hypothesis that the occasion of the color in the one case is a present external object, whereas the occasion in the case of dreams and hallucinations is of some other order such as a nerve stimulus of an obscure kind. In ordinary discourse the former definition, the external or objective view, generally prevails. The rose is said to be red, the coffee fragrant, the sugar sweet, and so forth; and the senory organs are said to apprehend the qualities, which are there, regardless of being apprehended. On this objective definition dualistic realism is again the explanation of the difference between the experience of a rose and the experience of a dream or hallucination.

A difficulty arises when we consider scientifically the physico-chemical situation which gives occasion to the experience of color. It is all very simple if color pigments and sounds are unanalyzed data, but the vibration which the physicist says takes place when we say we see red is so utterly different from the experience of color, and the vibration in the air set up by a violin string is so utterly different from the experience of sound, that we find it difficult to continue to call the physico-chemical situations by the old names, color and sound. Is this what color and sound "really" are? We may be hardheaded and simply stick to the old definition and say, "Yes, that is what they really are."

(b) A Third Definition

Perhaps, however, a third definition may be found in conformity with established usage, and may be better suited to a scientific view of physical and chemical situations: Qualities apprehended by the senses are *relationships, potential or actual, between physico-chemical situations and consciousness.* On this definition the rose is "really" red, but it is red *because* its physico-chemical state is such as to be the occasion for the experience of red when it is presented in ordinary light to ordinary conscious beings through ordinary sense organs. This definition leaves room for the fact that the same physico-chemical situation may be apprehended by instruments other than ordinary sense organs and may not then be the occasion for the experience of red.

(c) Opposing Philosophies

Idealists and experimentalists generally disagree with the suggestions outlined above. Idealists hold that all qualities exist only in and for minds or Mind; and experimentalists, denying mind and all other substantive entities, hold that the redness of the rose is simply an aspect of an event. In the on-going of experience (not the experience of a mind, they say, but just experience) an event occurs which is called a rose. Redness is a quality of this event, and that is all there is to it. This is essentially the position of William R. Dennes in his chapter "The Categories of Naturalism" in *Naturalism and the Human Spirit* (Columbia University Press, 1944).

(d) Dualistic Realist Assumption

In spite of these adverse opinions, it is here assumed that qualities are always qualities *of* — that is, that qualities always lead us to infer the existence of that of which they are qualities. This is the dualistic realist position, and I think we are justified in holding that this position is a basic assumption in the background of ordinary human discourse whenever the category of quality is involved.

(4) Other Kinds of Qualities

We have mentioned three kinds of qualities, definitive, additive and sensory. Obviously these classifications overlap. There are many other classes of qualities, such as personal, ethical, aesthetic, and so on, each classification depending upon a particular point of view. Valuational qualities are sometimes called tertiary, as distinguished from primary (definitive) and secondary (additive) qualities.

I. *The Category of Quantity*

The category of quantity is like the category of quality in that it usually leads to the preposition *of*. We ordinarily speak of the quantity of material substances, the quantity of time, the quantity (or volume) of sound, the quantity (or intensity) of light. However, quantity is usually regarded as a major category, and not just as a kind of quality or attribute.

Many *qualities* are sometimes considered abstractly. In studying ethics, for example, the nature of honesty in the abstract comes under consideration. But the category of *quantity* is conspicuous for the fact that numerous systems have been elaborated for the purpose of measuring it in the abstract. Geometry is largely devoted to the study of abstract quantitative relationships in space. A particular quart measure is a concrete object, but *a quart* is an abstraction which can be predicated of any fluid. A one mile track is concrete, but *a mile* is an abstraction. The revolutions of the hands of a clock, or of the earth on its axis, are concrete events, but *an hour* and *a day* are abstract concepts.

J. *The Category of Number*[17]

One of the most significant systems for the purpose of measuring quantity is arithmetic, or the science of numbers.

[17]In Kant's *Prolegomena*, section eleven, he says, "The pure intuition of space constitutes the basis of geometry — even arithmetic brings about its numerical conceptions by the successive addition of units in time; but above all, pure mechanics can evolve its conception of motion solely with the aid of the presentation of time." I agree with this opinion in regard to geometry and pure mechanics, but I am inclined to think that the category of *number* is a concept independent of the category of time.

The category of *number*, however, is not just a subheading under the category of quantity. In mere quantitative thinking, "One plus one equals more." As soon as we say, "One plus one equals two," we have passed into a realm of thought, or a category, of *number*, in which units are recognized as distinct, and capable of being identified as such.

(1) What Is a Unit?

Briefly, *a unit is whatever the mind takes for a whole,* or a total thing. This definition is not intended to deny that units exist in nature, whether we think of them or not. Certainly there are individual grains of sand, individual mountains, individual people and animals. The point is that for the category of number, units are taken as such by the mind, and it makes no difference in arithmetic whether the things designated be divided, or dissolved, or blown away by the wind. We may start home from the store with two packages of cereal, one carton of eggs, and two packages of cookies. We count, two plus one plus two equals five. We have five items which our minds identify as units. On the way home a package of cereal may be punctured and the contents leak out; one package may be lost; three eggs may be broken; and the cookies may be shattered to crumbs. We do not arrive at home with five items. What we physically retain is altered, but this does not make the slightest difference to our equation. Two plus one plus two still equals five. Units are taken as units by the mind, no matter how they may actually be divided or otherwise changed.

(2) What Are Numbers?

In discussing the category of time we studied Aristotle's comparison between time and number. We quoted him as saying, "Number is of two kinds, that which is counted, and that with which we count. . . . Number, e.g., ten, is the number of these horses, and so in other cases" (*Physics*, Book IV, Sections 219 b and 220 a). It was indicated that in regarding time as analogous to number in the sense of "that which is counted," Aristotle seems to have introduced confusion rather than clarification.

As for the category of number, Aristotle is perfectly right in saying, "Number is of two kinds, that which is counted, and that with which we count." But if the former meaning is taken, "that which is counted" — if "ten" means "these horses" — then we are essentially in the category of the substantive entities counted, that is, horses or what not. For the purpose of clarifying the category of number, it will be far more fruitful to take Aristotle's second meaning, "that with which we count." So we define the category of number as the abstract system by which we identify units and groupings or divisions of units. In other words, arithmetic, the science of the category of number, is that system of abstractions with which we manipulate units, add, subtract, multiply or divide; or, as Aristotle said, that with which we count.

(3) The Paradox[18] of Infinity

In recent philosophical discussions one frequently hears that since the sum of all numbers equals infinity, and the sum of all odd numbers also equals infinity, as well as the sum of all even numbers, and the sum of all prime numbers, therefore the old saying that a *whole* is greater than any of its *parts* is not true. The fallacy of this so-called paradox ought to be quite transparent. It is an intellectual outrage to consider infinity as a "whole." Infinity is neither a whole nor a sum.

A similar paradox is sometimes presented by drawing a long line and a short line on the blackboard and then saying, "There are just as many points in the short line as there are in the long line and therefore the long line is equal to the short line, which is one of its parts." This paradox is readily answered if the student remembers that points are not parts of lines. We do conceive of an infinite number of points in any line but the points are zero in extension. Infinity times zero is zero. Points do not make lines either long or short.

K. *The Category of Causation*

One of the most important and troublesome of the categories has to do with the matter of cause and effect. The two

[18]See discussion of similar paradoxes in sections on space and time above.

terms are correlative in usage. If A is the cause of B, then B is the effect of A.

(1) Origin of the Idea

We doubtless get the idea of causation from our own experience. Charles Hodge (1797-1878) argues that the notion of a substantive entity with power adequate for producing its effects is plain "from our own consciousness. We are causes. We can produce effects. . . . We are real existences; we have power; we have power adequate to the effects which we produce" *(Systematic Theology,* Vol. I, p. 209). F. R. Tennant argues similarly that the idea of causation results from "ejection of that subjectivity *erlebt* [experienced] by oneself, into bodies behaving like our own." Further he says, ". . . psychology can now suggest no possible origination of the category of efficient cause, save that of projection into the not-self, of what we experience when acting and acted upon. Effectuation [causing effects] is an ultimate, the notion of which could no more be forthcoming, unless the process were *erlebt,* than that of blue, unless blue were sensed" *(Philosophical Theology,* Vol. I, pp. 74 and 180).

This same thought was developed by John Locke (1632-1704) in his *Essay Concerning Human Understanding*[19] in a chapter entitled "Of Power." Locke says, "The idea of the beginning of motion we have only from reflection on what passes in ourselves, where we find by experience, that barely by willing it, barely by a thought of the mind, we can move the parts of our bodies which were before at rest. . . . But when I turn my eyes another way, or remove my body out of the sunbeams, I am properly active; because of my own choice, by a power within myself, I put myself into that motion. Such an action is the product of active power."

David Hume (1711-1776) in his *Inquiry Concerning Human Understanding,* Section 7, Part I, unsuccessfully attempts to answer Locke on this point.[20]

It should be noted that in discussing the origin of the

[19]Book II, Chapter XXI, Paragraphs 73 and 74.
[20]See my discussion of Hume on this point in *Philosophies of F. R. Tennant and John Dewey,* Philosophical Library, 1950, pp. 28 f.

idea of causation as expressed in human discourse, we are not passing any judgment upon the Kantian view that causation is an *a priori* category essential to the structure of our minds. When we come to the discussion of epistemology it will be necessary to consider the *a priori* rational structure of the mind. The question, for the present, is merely the nature of the idea as formulated in common literature.

(2) What Is Causation?
(a) Not the Sequence of Events

Causation is not what Hume took it to be, mere sequence of events in time. Charles Hodge, in the context of the passage quoted above, points out that although day follows night and night follows day, nobody supposes that day is the cause of night or that night is the cause of day. The seasons continue in their regular sequence, spring, summer, autumn, winter, but no one imagines that they successively cause one another.

(b) Not Logical Implication

The idea of logical implication has been substituted for the idea of causation by some rationalistic philosophers, but in ordinary discourse the difference is quite apparent. The relationship of the conclusion of a syllogism to the major and minor premises is not the same as the relationship of effect to cause. If all A is B, and all B is C, then it follows by the mere definition of the terms involved, and without any exercise of efficiency, that all A is C. This relationship of logical implication is obviously entirely different from the casual relationship implied, for example, in the statement, "Alcohol causes drunkenness."

(c) Not Only Mechanical Necessity

This is not the place to discuss psychological determinism or free will, but it is an appropriate place to point out that the idea of causation in human discourse is not identical with the idea of mechanical causation. Indeed, mechanical causation is not excluded. It is the power of the mainspring which causes the hands of the watch to revolve.

F.R. Tennant[21] discusses certain paradoxes of mechanical causality. If it is remembered that all mechanical causality involves movement in space and time, it will readily be seen that the paradoxes of mechanical causality are really identical with Zeno's paradoxes discussed above.

Mechanical causation is only a subdivision of the common usage of this category. We say with equal clarity it was the signal given over the radio which caused the man to set his clock in a certain way. Also it was the decision of the man to set his clock "correctly" which caused him to listen for the radio signal.

(d) The Idea of Effective Power

If we carefully analyze the various usages of causation in human discourse, we shall discover that the basic idea involved is some kind of power, energy, potentiality or efficiency, brought to bear upon a situation in such a way as to produce a result, or an effect.

(3) Kinds of Causation

Aristotle's four kinds of cause are frequently referred to. These are discussed in his *Physics*, Book II, Chapter III, in his *Metaphyiscs*, Book IV, Chapter II, and elsewhere. "Material cause" is the material of which an object is made, or the classification to which it belongs. Bronze is the material cause of a bronze statue and silver is the material cause of a silver bowl. Both of these belong to the general classification of metals. "Formal cause" is the essence or definition or complex of essential attributes of an object. "Efficient cause" is the active agent which brings about the effect. The "final cause" is the purpose of the effect, or that for which it is brought about.

It is customary to add to these four causes two more, "proximate cause" and "remote cause." The chisel of the sculptor is the proximate cause of the form of the marble statue, but the plan or purpose of the statue is the remote cause.

[21]Article on "Causality" in Hastings' *Encyclopaedia of Religion and Ethics*, Vol. III, pp. 261 ff.

Obviously there is much overlapping between these kinds of causes, and each kind of cause may be extremely complex. For example, the efficient cause of any event may be the entire chain of circumstances leading up to it.

It is my feeling that still another classification is necessary. In the study of subjects in which either value or disvalue is attached by the human mind to events or to objects, we frequently ask, "What is *the* cause?" But of course, merely to emphasize the definite article still leaves the question ambiguous. I suggest that the terms, "creditable cause," or "chargeable cause," would greatly clarify any discussion of causation connected with values.

Thus, in Christian theology we say that the only *creditable cause* of the salvation of a sinner is the grace of God.[22] On the other hand we say that the *chargeable cause* of the eternal loss of a sinner is his rejection of the Saviour.[23]

(4) Is Causation Universal?

The notion that causality is absolutely universal has been held by some of the greatest thinkers in our history. This question will come up again in our discussion of dualistic realism in metaphysics. (See pages 147-160). There is some necessary repetition. The present purpose is to acquaint the student with the common use of terms.

(a) Rationalist View

Among the rationalists there are many who adhere to the Latin formula *ratio est causa essendi*, reason is the cause of being. In the above discussion we have indicated that reason, in the sense of logic, is not the same as cause. But still a multitude of the rationalists are not convinced. Leibnitz (1646-1716) announced what he called "the law of sufficient reason." D. S. Robinson of the University of Southern California quotes Leibnitz as follows: "No fact can be found real or existing, no statement true, unless there be a sufficient reason why it should be so and not otherwise."[24] Robinson

[22]Ephesians 2:8-10.
[23]John 3:18, 19.
[24]*The Principles of Reasoning,* third edition, 1947, p. 366.

then paraphrases the law of sufficient reason in his own words, "For everything that exists or is real we must assume that there is a full explanation or reason for its being what it is rather than otherwise from what it actually is." This matter was referred to in Chapter I in connection with the relationship between logic and metaphysics. See page 22 ff.

This law of sufficient reason is held in connection with the theory that the entire universe is "an implicative system." Robinson says, "This conception of an inferential whole, or an implicative system, is employed again and again throughout this textbook, and the student will do well to grasp it here at the outset."[25] Later he explains, ". . . in reality everything is what it is because of its place in the system."[26]

Assuming that reason is the cause of being, Robinson holds to a rigid law of universal causation. He says, ". . . according to this law or principle, every event which happens in the Universe is the result of some previous event or events, without which it could not have happened, and with which being present, it must happen."[27]

This theory of a rigid totalitarian causal system is held by Professor Stuart C. Hackett of Louisiana College. Professor Hackett is a devout Christian scholar. His recent book, *The Resurrection of Theism*[28] sets forth his theory of "rational empiricism."

(b) The Mechanistic View

Believers in a rigid totalitarian causal system are found not only among the rationalists, but also among those who hold other types of philosophy. The so-called mechanistic view of the universe is generally inconsistent with the rationalistic definition of causation. It is not necessarily connected with, but is consistent with the definition of causation which we have defended above. According to the mechanistic view, everything in the universe is totally bound up in a causal system, as though the total were a vast machine. All phenomena, physical, chemical, biological, psychological, ethical,

[25]*Ibid.*, pp. 8 f.
[26]*Ibid.*, pp. 336 f.
[27]*Ibid.*, p. 253.
[28]Moody Press, 1957.

aesthetic, spiritual — all phenomena of every kind are held to be mechanically determined. This mechanistic theory is frequently called "determinism" in the field of psychology, but the words mechanism and determinism are practically interchangeable.

The mechanistic view is put into words by Laplace (1749-1827), the noted French astronomer and mathematician. Laplace said, "If an intelligence, for one given instant, recognizes all the forces which animate Nature, and the respective positions of the things which compose it, and if that intelligence is also sufficiently vast to subject these data to analysis, it will comprehend in one formula the movements of the largest bodies of the universe as well as those of the minutest atom: nothing will be uncertain to it, and the future as well as the past will be present to its vision. The human mind offers in the perfection which it has been able to give to astronomy, a modest example of such an intelligence."[29] Cajori comments, "In these words we have a bold assertion of the belief in determinism . . . In answer to a question whether it was true that in his *Mecanique celeste* he had never mentioned the Creator, Laplace told Napoleon, *'Je n'avais pas besoin de cette hypothese-là'* [I have not had need of this hypothesis]."[30]

Such was not the view of Sir Isaac Newton (1642-1727). Cajori says of Newton, ". . . he did not believe that there was a 'world machine' which kept on running according to the law of gravitation without supervision of God, but rather that irregularities in the solar system caused by action of planets and comets on each other are regulated by God whenever emergencies arise. 'This most beautiful system of the sun, planets and comets,' says Newton in his *Principia* (Book III, Proposition 42, General Scholium) 'could only proceed from the counsel and dominion of an intelligent and powerful Being.' "[31]

[29]Quoted by Florian Cajori in his 1946 edition of Newton's *Principia*. Appendix, p. 677. The quotation is from Laplace's *Essai Philosophique sur les Probabilités*, from Laplace's complete *Works* in French, Volume 7, p. 6.
[30]*Idem.*
[31]*Idem.*

(5) Opposition to Universal Causation

Opposition to the theory of total universal causation may be observed in two very different philosophical camps: the camp of the emergentists and the camp of the theists.

(a) Emergentism

As a strange reaction against extreme mechanism or determinism, there are influential thinkers today who frankly hold that finite beings or events can come into existence without any cause whatsoever. They emphatically deny the old saying, *"ex nihilo nihil fit,"* "from nothing nothing comes." One such thinker who has put the matter bluntly is Fred Hoyle, a physicist, Fellow of St. John's College, Cambridge, England. In his small book, *The Nature of the Universe,*[32] he frankly recognizes that modern physics indicates that the material universe had a beginning. He bluntly rejects the Biblical doctrine of the creation of the universe by an eternal Personal Intelligence. As an alternative theory he holds that hydrogen atoms are continuously coming into existence from nothing, by nothing, without any cause whatsoever. He thinks that this emergence of hydrogen atoms, uncaused, is the force which drives the material universe along. Professor Sidney Hook of New York University, whose views might be called neo-materialistic, is also one of a group holding to materialistic emergentism. So far as I know he has not elaborated his views as Fred Hoyle has done.

(b) The Theistic View

Those who believe in the Biblical doctrine of the creation of the universe by a Personal Intelligence reject both the notion of an absolutely rigid total causal system, and the notion that anything can come from nothing, that is that anything can come into being without a cause. Accepting the view that from nothing nothing comes, theists point out that if anything does now exist (as the universe certainly does) then something must be eternal. We argue that atheistic materialism must come to the same conclusion, if it does not accept the

---

[32]Harper's, 1950. Hoyle's views are more fully discussed below in the chapter on "Materialism." See also Hoyle's *Frontiers of Astronomy*, Mentor, Harper's, 1957.

absurdity of something coming from nothing. The atheistic materialist may hold that the physical universe is eternal, but even so the causal series of events in the eternal past does not explain the existence of the universe, the series of events as a series. If the material universe is eternal, then it is, in itself, as an eternal series, something which has no cause. The theist argues that it is much more reasonable to believe in an eternal uncaused Personal Intelligence than to believe in any other eternal uncaused being.

It should be made clear that the theist is not at all interested in denying the universality of causation within the material universe. The theist simply holds that since the existence of anything at all proves that there must be some eternal uncaused being, and since modern physics indicates that the material universe has had a beginning, it is far more reasonable to believe that God is the eternal uncaused Being.

The theist of course believes in personal causation as well as mechanical causation. It should be clear that the Biblical doctrine of creation is not the doctrine of something coming from nothing without a cause, but it is the doctrine of the origination of the finite universe by a personal eternal Cause.

L. *The Category of States of Consciousness*

Lengthy discussion will not be necessary, but it is important in connection with the study of the categories to call attention to the fact that much of human discourse is concerned with states of consciousness. We are not only aware of objects and events, but we are also aware of our awareness. Older psychologists sometimes classified states of consciousness in three divisions, intellect, emotion and will. Technical names for these divisions are cognition, affection and conation. These divisions may be accepted as roughly descriptive of mental activity, but phychologists find many subdivisions under each heading.

Without attempting to elaborate the divisions and subdivisions of states of consciousness, it will be valuable at this point to call attention to three types of mental images which human beings frequently discuss. These are perceptual images, memory images and imaginative images. It is important not only for the philosopher but also for the simple man of affairs to distinguish between the images of actual perception and the images of memory and imagination.

M. *The Category of Value*

A vast amount of human discourse is concerned with various kinds of value. We have indicated in Chapter I that logic is concerned with truth value, aesthetics is concerned with beauty value, and ethics is concerned with the value of goodness or rightness. These three normative sciences are far from exhausting the subject of value. For example, much of the material covered in economics is concerned with what the economists call exchange value. It goes without saying that whatever goods one desires to the extent that he is willing to pay a price in exchange for them, are valued for the reason of some other value. If the individual is purchasing goods for sale, he exchanges money, or other goods, for the sake of further exchange value in the form of profit. If the individual desires the goods to eat or to wear, he exchanges his money or his goods for the sake of food value or physical comfort value. Whenever exchange is voluntarily consummated, the total value for the parties to the exchange is increased. Each party values what he gives less than what he gets, or otherwise the exchange would not take place.

It is not necessary to elaborate the many kinds of value about which human beings speak and write. But it is important to call the philosophy student's attention to the fact that he should know what particular kind of value he has in mind when he ventures into the category of valuation.

N. *The Category of Being*

The literature on the subject of being is vast and the confusion is appalling. Since the section on ontology is in itself a study of the theory of being, we need not here engage in any lengthy discussion of the many views which are held.

It is the opinion of the present writer that the category of being is essentially a category of other categories, and is not a category in itself. In other words, I suggest that all forms of the verb "to be" and of the verb "to exist"[33] (as well as other words of similar usage, such as "reality"), if used intelligibly, assert or imply the being of something in some category other than mere being.

It is a commonplace observation[34] among students of philosophy that the verb "to be" is both a copula and a predicate. Sometimes the word denotes existence, and sometimes, grammatically, the word simply connects a subject with its attributes or its activities. My contention is that whether the verb "to be" is a copula or a predicate, in any case it always implies a copulative relationship with some category other than being.

The reader will doubtless object that the words, "God is," have quite a different meaning from the words, "God is good." It is argued that the second of these sentences could refer to an imaginary being, whereas the first could not. In this I agree, but still I would argue that the words, "God is," do not refer to mere existence as such, but in each particular cultural horizon they have a meaning in some other category than mere being. For example, in the horizon of the Judeo-Christian tradition the words "God is" clearly mean the God described in the Bible exists as a substantive entity, a non-material spiritual Person, "infinite, eternal and unchangeable in His being, wisdom, power, holiness, justice, goodness and truth." This is much more than a category of "pure being."

I fully realize that the suggestion that there is no such category as pure being in intelligible thought, is quite revolutionary. Those who object will call attention to the writings of Thomas Aquinas and a vast amount of neo-Thomistic literature. I am well aware that the Thomists hold that God is "Pure Being" and that God is not in any genus or category,

---

[33]For a discussion of the ambiguity of "existence" see a clever article entitled "Logic and Ontology" by Bertrand Russell in the *Journal of Philosophy* for April 25, 1957. Russell illustrates the difficulties by the following sentence: "Whether Romulus existed is doubtful, since reasons exist for questioning the reliability of existing legends as to the first century of Rome's existence."
[34]Kant, *Kritik der reinen Vernunft,* Tt. Dial. Bk. II, Ch. II, Sec. IV. *"Sein ist offenbar kein reales Prädikat. . . . Im logischen Gebrauch ist es lediglich die Copula eines Urtheils."* ("The verb 'to be' is often no real predicate. . . . In logical usage it is purely the copula of a judgment.")

whatsoever. My contention is that such statements are mere combinations of syllables without intelligible connotation. A god who is not a non-material substantive entity, is not the God whom Thomas Aquinas intended to describe. A god who is not "a spirit" in the genus spirit, in whose image we, as human spirits, are created, is either a creature of imagination or in some other category in some other cultural horizon than our own. In spite of the fact that I know many philosophers will reject the suggestion on the first reading, I still insist that the words "pure being" are absurd.

What is said here with reference to being and existing is true also of combinations of the word real and reality. We may say, for example, "I really dreamed it; I didn't make it up." Usually the word "real" means real as a substantive entity, but this is not always the case. Real may mean real in any category.

A word of caution is in order on the subject of the figurative uses of negative forms of the word being. All will doubtless recognize that "to be a non entity" in ordinary discourse does not mean to be literally non-existent. So "to be a nobody" is not taken literally. It is merely a depreciatory remark. A large department store in New York City has had the slogan "Nobody But Nobody Undersells Gimbels." When a customer calls the management's attention to the fact that certain other merchants undersell particular items, the reply is, "Oh, they are Nobody."

All this would be quite obvious, except that in existential philosophy[35] a great number of students work up an intense emotional state of *Angst und Sorge*[36] over the question of "non-being." Perhaps the existentialist might snap out of it if he would only ask himself, "Non-being in what category?"

[35]On the existential theology of Paul Tillich see the publications of two of my colleagues: Dr. R. Allen Killen *The Ontological Theology of Paul Tillich,* Kampen, Holland, 1956, and Dr. William W. Paul, *Paul Tillich's Interpretation of History,* Columbia University, Microfilm Service, 1959. See also Dr. Paul's review of a book in honor of Tillich in the *Journal of Philosophy* for Oct. 8, 1959, pp. 837-842.

[36]These German words are not easy to translate, but, roughly, the phrase means "concern and grief."

O. *Other Categories*

There are many other categories in human discourse, some of them of great importance. We have discussed in this chapter some of the most troublesome ones, some in which there is much ambiguity in current usage.

We may well close this chapter by reiterating an admonition given at the beginning: Know what you are saying. Be clear, in all speaking and writing, in what category your predications lie.

PART II

ONTOLOGY, THE THEORY OF BEING

CHAPTER III

MATERIALISM

A. *Definition*

Materialism is a term which includes those types of metaphysics, or ontology, which regard all substantive entities as composed of matter, or space-occupying bodies. This definition, like many others, is controversial. There are materialists who will object. Nevertheless, the student will find that if this definition is strictly adhered to, the various types of materialistic philosophy may be intelligibly catalogued and reasonably understood.

(1) A Theory of Being

Note that materialism is a kind of ontology, a theory of being, not a theory of knowing. Materialists must somehow take account of knowing. This statement is true even of those types of materialism which deny or ignore consciousness. Their denial or their ignoring is a way of accounting for the knowing process, if we may stretch the word "accounting" to include the process of "writing off" assets alleged to have no value. The materialist has a theory of knowing, or an epistemology, but his epistemology is not the same thing as his materialism.

Some types of materialism attempt to account for knowing on the theory that the knower, *res cogitans,* is made up of extended things, *res extensa.* In so-called primitive religions, the thinking thing is frequently accounted for by a materialistic notion of the soul.[1] At a recent meeting of the Eastern Division of the American Philosophical Association, Professor Edel argued that intellectual activity is not to be taken as evidence against materialism. "The fact that we are here reading philosophical papers to one another simply proves that atoms, space occupying entities, are capable of being so

[1]See the article "Soul, Primitive," by H. B. Alexander in *Hastings' Encyclopaedia of Religion and Ethics,* Vol. XI, p. 725.

69

arranged as to be able to assemble and read philosophical papers to one another."[2]

(2) Space-Occupying

Note that the only specified attribute of the components of substantive entities, according to materialism, is that these components occupy space. Materialists may accept an atomic theory, but they are not confined to any atomic theory, ancient or modern. Some materialists have held that the substance of which all things are made is electricity, and that electricity is essentially non-molecular, or non-atomic. They think of such entities as electrons as analogous to vortices in a fluid. There are materialists who reject the so-called law of the conservation of matter, that is, there are those who believe that matter may go out of existence. The same kind of doubt is held with reference to the so-called law of the conservation of energy. There are also many materialists today who believe that matter and energy are interchangeable, that is, that matter may be converted into energy and that energy may be converted into matter. These theories, however, are not a part of the definition of materialism, as such.

(3) Plausibility

The student will recognize that materialism, as above-defined, has a kind of natural appeal to the ordinary mind. We are accustomed to taking material things and putting them together to form material products. We know that matter is exceedingly complex and versatile. We know that our own bodies are made up of space-occupying parts. The theory that all things are thus composed is easy to accept on a superficial view.

(4) Implicit Materialism

In giving the definition above, it was indicated that this definition should be adhered to "strictly." It must be recognized, however, that there are types of materialism which are implicit rather than explicit. There are important writers who would prefer not to be classed as materialists who nevertheless avoid a clear-cut affirmation of non-material substantive

[2]The quotation is not verbatim, but accurate for substance.

entities, such as the soul or God. Moreover, there are those who give lip service to non-material substantive entities in their religious language but who make it sufficiently plain that they regard such religious language as merely figurative or symbolical.

B. *Historical Systems of Materialism*

(1) Biblical Writings and Materialism

The Judeo-Christian Scriptures do not indicate that the Hebrew people had contacts with those who held explicitly to a materialistic philosophy. The religious and speculative ideas of the Egyptians and the Babylonians were animistic and polytheistic. A background assumption with reference to souls and gods may have been crudely materialistic in some instances, but we do not find any explicit reaction to any ethnic teaching to that effect.

What we do find in the Bible is an emphasis upon the relative unimportance of material things, in perspective. They are only a *part* of metaphysical reality. The Book of Proverbs is monumental as a work in the field of economics. In the New Testament Paul teaches, "Let him that stole steal no more: but rather let him labour, working with his hands the thing which is good, that he may have to give to him that needeth."[3] The prophets and the apostles of the Judeo-Christian Scriptures frequently describe and condemn a kind of implicit materialism which places disproportionate emphasis upon material things, and forgets the things of the spirit. In the words of Jesus, "Is not the life more than meat, and the body than raiment? . . . But seek ye first the kingdom of God and his righteousness; and all these things shall be added unto you."[4]

(2) Democritus and the Atomists

The first system of materialistic philosophy in recorded human culture is that elaborated by Democritus (approximately 460-362 B.C.) and the Greek atomists who followed his philosophy. Democritus was a contemporary of Socrates, who

[3]Ephesians 4:28.
[4]Matthew 6:25, 33.

was put to death in 399 B.C. Democritus however does not belong in the great tradition of Socrates, Plato and Aristotle. We have no extended writings of Democritus such as we have of Plato and of Aristotle; and we have no biography or extended biographical data such as we have of Socrates in Plato's *Apology* and Xenophon's *Memorabilia*. For Democritus we have only brief quotations and allusions in the classical writers; but classical scholars have done an extensive amount of research in reconstructing something of his philosophy.[5]

Although our knowledge of the life of Democritus comes almost entirely from traditions which cannot be completely verified, yet the evidence we have seems to indicate that he was truly a great intellect and a great philosopher. The outstanding feature of his metaphysics is the doctrine that all things are made of atoms. We have, he thinks, only two ontological factors to reckon with, atoms, and empty space.

However, Democritus' atoms were different from the atoms of modern physics. The Greek word *atome* means "uncuttable" or "indivisible." The atoms were supposed to be the indivisible units of which all matter is composed. They were believed to fill the space they occupied absolutely, with not the slightest intra-atomic space. This conception of the atom is to be contrasted with the modern idea, according to which the unoccupied space inside an atom is greater, proportionately, than the space inside the solar system compared with

[5]An extensive study of the philosophy of Democritus, and the development of it in the philosophy of Epicurus and Lucretius is found in *The History of Materialism* by Frederick Albert Lange, second German edition, 1875. English translation is by Ernest Chester Thomas, third English edition, 1925, with introduction by Bertrand Russell, three volumes in one.

I would earnestly recommend that the beginning student form the encyclopedia habit early in the study of philosophy. The articles on Democritus, Epicurus, Lucretius, Materialism, and other topics of importance, will give the beginner a critically oriented starting point. If the student does not know where to start, in any field of general learning, I would recommend the *Encyclopaedia Britannica*. The student will there find at least a general historical article and a bibliography on whatever subject he wishes to investigate. Later he will learn the specialized encyclopedias and dictionaries and from there go on to the great monographs. Of course, in philosophy the greatest dictionary (up to 1902) is Baldwin's three volume work, *The Dictionary of Philosophy and Psychology* recently reprinted by Peter Smyth, New York. Runes' *Dictionary of Philosophy* is much less extensive but includes recent topics and important names up to the 1940's.

the macroscopically solid matter. The atoms were held to differ from one another in quantity and combinations only, not in quality. Matter and its motion (force) are explained by the concept of innumerable atoms falling eternally through infinite space. The heavier atoms would thus fall more rapidly (contrary to the discoveries of modern physics) and would overtake and collide with the lighter atoms, setting up innumerable lateral motions and vortices, and giving rise to the material objects in the world of experience. All the behavior of the atoms was thought to be governed by inflexible mechanical laws.

Democritus did not carry out his mechanistic views in such a manner as to deny the existence of human souls, or supernatural beings; nor did he deny consciousness or personal ethical responsibility. The soul, he held, is composed of a particularly fine, smooth, mobile kind of atoms. These he identified with fire atoms floating in the air. The soul is replenished by inhaling, and depleted by exhaling. When breathing stops, the soul is gone. Students of the Democritus philosophy argue that personal immortality was denied by his atomic theory of the soul, but this seems to be a modern inference rather than a recorded doctrine of Democritus himself.

Democritus believed in the existence of supernatural beings, the popularly recognized pagan gods of Greece. He held that they did not create or govern the universe, but that they do communicate with men. The gods were thought to be composed of subtle atoms, and thus they were less subject to disintegration than human souls.

The sensations of consciousness were explained by the theory of the throwing off of subtle atoms from the surface of physical objects in the form of emanations or images which impinge upon the appropriate sense organs, and thus upon the soul. Democritus anticipated Locke's distinction between primary qualities such as extension and mass, and secondary qualities such as color. The latter, said Democritus, are derived from the impingement of various configurations of atoms upon the soul.

In ethics the teachings of Democritus are hedonistic.

Pleasure is the criterion of the good. True pleasure, however, is not sensuous enjoyment, but tranquility of the soul. Extremes must be avoided.

(3) Epicurean Materialism

The materialism of Democritus was carried forward by Epicurus (342-270 B.C.) and by the Latin Epicurean poet, Lucretius (about 98-55 B.C.).

We have much more information concerning the metaphysics of the Epicureans than we have for Democritus, but the Epicureans seem to have followed Democritus closely. The most important metaphysical advance was in the theory that the atoms are possessed of a certain degree of free will, so that they may voluntarily change their course as they proceed through infinite space. Lange[6] finds the doctrine of the free will of the atoms in both Epicurus and Lucretius.

It is interesting that a theory of astronomical spheres, even in this early day, had led to the questioning of Democritus' notion of "falling" through infinite space. According to the theory of spheres, the word "falling" would have no meaning, since the direction up-and-down would be indeterminate in astronomical space. The notion of up-and-down being determined by the center of the spherical earth had not yet arisen.

This question was easily answered by the Epicureans by the simple fact that the "direction from my head to my feet" is still determinate, even in a universe of spheres. The atoms, accordingly, follow the direction from man's head to his feet in their eternal motion.

The Epicureans did not deny the existence of the soul, though Lucretius argued emphatically that the soul is not immortal. Neither did they deny the existence of the pagan gods. They did vigorously deny that the gods interfere with or are concerned about human affairs on the earth. Lucretius is called an atheist, but this accusation is probably unjust. He argues sarcastically against the superstitious ideas which were prevalent in the world of his day, but he devoutly in-

[6]*Op cit.*, Vol. I, p. 141, note 68.

vokes the assistance of Divinity. Some students of ancient philosophy argue that Lucretius believed in the supreme God over all, a world-pervading Spirit. It is thought that he may have gained such a concept from Democritus' notion of the universality of the atoms of which souls are created. It must be admitted that the notion of a universal divine Spirit is not at all clear either in Democritus or in Lucretius.

(4) Stoic Materialism

Lange[7] questions the genuineness of the materialism of the Stoics. He says, ". . . the distinctive feature of Materialism is here wanting — the purely material nature of matter; the origination of all phenomena, including those of adaptation and spirit, through movements of matter according to universal laws of motion." It may be argued, however, that Lange's objection to Stoic materialism may be applied to any system of materialism which the history of philosophy can reveal. Robert Flint,[8] in his excellent chapters on materialism, illustrates the fact. He says (p. 42), "It is a universal characteristic of materialism that it supposes matter to be more than it is known to be; that it imaginatively exalts and glorifies matter beyond what sense or science warrants. It always attributes to matter eternity and self-existence; sometimes it supposes it to be likewise essentially active; sometimes it endows it with life, with sensation, with volition, with intelligence. Systems which agree in verbally representing matter as the foundation and explanation of the universe, differ enormously as to what matter is, but they all, without exception, ascribe to matter properties of which experience teaches us nothing."

Stoicism was founded in Greece by Zeno (about 336-264 B.C.) and continued, chiefly in Rome, until the time of Marcus Aurelius (121-180). Lange[9] tells us that for the Stoic all things are composed of bodies. This includes not only the human soul, but the human virtues and emotions as well. The man who is said to be just "must have the substance of justice in his body."

[7]Op. cit., Vol. I, page 96.
[8]Anti-Theistic Theories, Edinburgh, fifth edition, 1894.
[9]Op. cit., Vol. I, pp. 96 ff.

The Stoic materialism was distinctly pantheistic. The world has a universal soul which governs all things.

Lange describes the situation: "The force of all forces . . . is the deity which permeates and moves the whole universe with its influence. . . . The Stoics, indeed, have no transcendental god, and no soul absolutely independent of body; yet their matter is thoroughly pervaded, and not merely influenced by soul; their god is identical with the world, yet he is more than self-moving matter; he is the 'fiery reason of the world,' and this reason works that which is reasonable and purposeful. . . ."[10]

The stoic psychology and ethics are rigidly deterministic.[11] "Moral accountability is involved in the fact that conduct flows from the will and so from the innermost and most essential nature of man; but the manner in which each man's will moves itself is only a result of the mighty necessity and divine predestination which govern all the machinery of the universe down to the smallest detail."[12]

(5) The Materialism of Thomas Hobbes
(1588-1679)

The philosophy of materialism in the ancient world comes to an end with the life of the Roman Emperor Marcus Aurelius. Robert Flint remarks, "A history of theoretical materialism in the middle ages could not be written, for the simple reason that there was none to write."[13]

With Thomas Hobbes in the seventeenth century we come to a distinctive type of materialism, the influence of which has continued to the present time. Lange[14] credits Gassendi (1592-1655) with stimulating Hobbes' materialism. Flint, however, thinks that Lange's account is "one-sided."[15] Flint describes Gassendi as a "learned and worthy priest." He argues that Gassendi taught that atoms are not eternal but were created *ex nihilo* by the Divine Will, that the soul is

[10]*Op. cit.*, Vol. I, pp. 96 ff.
[11]Determinism is the opposite of the doctrine of free will.
[12]*Ibid.*, p. 97.
[13]*Op. cit.*, p. 468.
[14]*Op. cit.*, Vol. I, pp. 253 ff.
[15]*Op. cit.*, pp. 469 ff.

immaterial and immortal. He makes Gassendi out to be rather one of the "rational assailants of materialism." It is clear that Gassendi was a personal friend of Hobbes, and also that Gassendi admired certain aspects of Epicurean philosophy, but it seems just as clear that he did not agree with Hobbes' doctrine that matter is the only metaphysical reality.

The life and the philosophy of Thomas Hobbes are both interesting and exasperating, but that story lies outside the purposes of the present work. He succeeded in riding out the storm of English and French politics of the mid-seventeenth century. He elaborated enormous absurdities in the field of mathematics. His extensive discussions of political theories seem scarcely less absurd. He evolved a vast system of materialistic thought, which, in his own mind, seemed entirely consistent with the Thirty Nine Articles of the official doctrine of the Church of England. It is this system of materialism which we must survey.

Hobbes' materialism may be summed up in a brief passage from *The Leviathan:* ". . . the *Universe,* that is to say, the whole masse of all things that are, is Corporeall, that is to say, body: and hath the dimensions of Magnitude, namely, Length, Bredth, and Depth: also every part of Body, is likewise Body, and hath the like dimensions; and consequently every part of the Universe, is Body; and that which is not Body, is no part of the Universe: And because the Universe is All, that which is no part of it, is *Nothing;* and consequently *nowhere"* (pp. 367 f.).[16]

One can scarcely imagine a more distinct statement of materialistic metaphysics. The same doctrine is elaborated throughout. (See especially pp. 211, 217, 370.)

Hobbes' doctrine of the human soul may be illustrated by references to *The Leviathan,* pages 337 and 241. The soul is nothing but the living body, or the life of the body, or the body while it is alive. At death the soul ceases to exist, but

[16]Hobbes' chief work, *The Leviathan,* was originally published in 1651. It has gone through many editions and is now available in an inexpensive binding in the "Everyman's Library," publication No. 691. Page references in the following quotations from Hobbes will be found in the Everyman's Library edition.

in the resurrection at the second coming of Christ, the body will be made alive and thus the soul will exist. Eternal life is obtainable only through the sacrifice of Christ. "Now Jesus Christ hath satisfied for the sins of all that believe in Him; and therefore recovered to all believers, that ETERNAL LIFE, which was lost by the sin of Adam" (p. 241). Eternal life consists in the restoration of physical life to the body at the resurrection, and will be enjoyed strictly upon this physical earth.

Although much of this is quite crudely inconsistent with Biblical teaching, yet Hobbes sometimes approaches genuine gospel doctrine. "All that is NECESSARY *to salvation* is contained in two vertues, *Faith in Christ,* and *Obedience to Laws.* The latter of these, if it were perfect, were enough to us. But because we are all guilty of disobedience to God's Law, not onely originally in Adam, but also actually by our own transgressions, there is required at our hands now, not onely *Obedience* for the rest of our time, but also a *Remission* of sins for the time past; which remission is the reward of our Faith in Christ. That nothing else is Necessarily required to Salvation, is manifest from this, that the Kingdom of Heaven is shut to none but to sinners; that is to say, to the disobedient, or transgressors of the Law; nor to them, in case they Repent and Believe all the Articles of the Christian Faith, Necessary to Salvation" (pp. 319 f.).

Lange says of Hobbes, ". . . it is bluntly said that *God rules only through nature,* and that His will is announced through the State. We must not indeed conclude from this that Hobbes identified God with the sum of nature — pantheistically. He seems rather to have conceived of God as a part of the Universe — controlling, universally spread, uniform, and by this motion determining mechanically the motion of the whole. As the history of the world is an outflow of natural laws, so the power of a State is, as the actual effective might, an outflow of the Divine will."[17]

In numerous passages Hobbes emphasizes his notion that all angels and spirits are corporeal bodies. He never, to my

[17]*Op. cit.,* Vol. I, p. 290, note.

knowledge, states that God is a material body, or that God is a part of the universe. In several instances, in connection with statements to the effect that all things that exist are corporeal, he makes an exception of the being of God by saying that "God is incomprehensible."

Lange suggests that Hobbes was hypocritical in his concessions to Christian doctrine. He says, "If one could have overheard a confidential conversation between Gassendi and Hobbes, one might perhaps have caught a dispute on the question whether the all-animating heat or the all-embracing ether must be regarded as the deity."[18] It must be remembered, however, that Lange is inclined to exaggerate the materialism of some of his subjects at the expense of their distinctly religious affirmations. Though Lange himself does not wholeheartedly accept materialism,[19] yet he is so sympathetic with materialism in its mechanistic form that Eduard von Hartmann describes his work as *eine durch geschichtliche Studien angeschwollene Tendenzschrift,*[20] "A controversial writing swollen up by historical studies."

Hobbes is sometimes classed as a deist and sometimes as an atheist, but neither of these classifications is correct. I remember reading in Robert Bailie's *Letters* written from London during the time of the Westminster Assembly (1643-1649), a volume not now available to me, a remark to the effect that it is a great pity that the "atheist" Thomas Hobbes had been made tutor to the Prince of Wales, that is, Charles II, who was then in exile in France. Professor John Orr in his useful work, *English Deism, Its Roots and Its Fruits,*[21] gives the impression that Hobbes is to be classed as a deist. In my opinion, Professor Orr is in error in this. Hobbes is belligerently loyal to the infallibility and authority of the Bible, and defines the canon of Scripture strictly in accordance with the Protestant view. His theology is erratic; in fact it is fantastic in many points, but I would urge that we have no grounds

[18]*Op. cit.,* Vol. I, page 290.
[19]Lange thought that materialism could not explain consciousness.
[20]Quoted by Ernest Chester Thomas in the Translator's Preface of the third English Edition.
[21]Eerdmans, 1934, pp. 70 ff.

to deny that he sincerely thought himself to be loyal to the Bible and to the official doctrines of the Church of England.

(6) Eighteenth Century Materialism

Materialism in England in the century following Thomas Hobbes was inconsequential, but, as Flint says, "It was only when transplanted from England to France, in the generation before the Revolution, that materialism grew up to maturity."[22]

Outstanding names among French materialists of the eighteenth century are listed by Flint as follows: "LaMettrie (1709-1784), . . . Von Holbach (1723-1789), Diderot (1713-1784), Helvetius (1717-1771), D'Alembert (1717-1783), Lalande (1732-1807), Naigeon (1738-1810), Condorcet (1743-1794) and Marechal (1750-1803). LaMettrie, Diderot, Helvetius and D'Alembert may be regarded as forming an earlier . . . group."[23] Von Holbach was the connecting link between the earlier and the later group.

Flint does not include Cabanis (1757-1808) but James Orr[24] quotes his famous saying, "The brain secretes thought as the liver secretes bile." Windelband in his *History of Philosophy* (p. 634) calls Cabanis "the leader of the *materialistic* line." Lange says of Cabanis that we find in his writings "nearly all the watchwords of our modern Materialists, as, e.g., the idea that *thoughts are a secretion of the brain*."[25] Lange here refers to Cabanis' "Rapports S.," p. 138.

Although the French materialism of the eighteenth century was philosophically barren and unoriginal, yet its importance in the history of western culture is great because of the religious and moral doctrines which these men claimed as corollaries of their philosophy.

(a) French materialism of the eighteenth century was blatantly, but inconsistently, atheistic. Of LaMettrie, Flint says, "It shows the mental calibre of the man that he should, in one sentence, say that it is very probable that there may

[22]*Op. cit.*, p. 82.
[23]*Op. cit.*, p. 470.
[24]*The Christian View*, p. 143.
[25]*Op. cit.*, Vol. II, p. 242.

be a God, and then, in those which immediately follow, that there are no grounds for believing in the existence of God — that even if there be a God, there is no need for us to have any religion — and that it is foolish to trouble ourselves as to whether there is a God or not. In one page he affirms that it is perfectly indifferent to our happiness whether God does or does not exist, and a few pages further on he is pleased to inform us that the world will never be happy till atheism is universal. It did not occur to him that although both of these assertions might very well be false, they certainly could not both be true."[26]

The same dogmatic, contradictory atheism is found in the writings of von Holbach and the rest of the group.

(b) The ethics of eighteenth century materialism in France exhibited great laxity. Flint says of Diderot, "He was the only morally worthy, or even morally decent man, belonging to the older atheistical group. Its three other members had some good qualities, but they were shamelessly impure, licentious, and untruthful."[27] As for von Holbach, "Many will think that from these premises he should have drawn the conclusion, there is no morality. He did not quite do that, for the man was greatly better than his system; but, of course, he could not inculcate a pure or high morality. He could only rest duty on self-interest."

Flint continues, "The moral principles advocated by La-Mettrie and Holbach were not peculiar to them. Helvetius, Saint Lambert, Morelly, and a host of other writers, likewise inculcated a more or less refined selfishness, as the sole sure basis both of ethical theory and ethical life. . . .

"When God was decreed a non-entity and death an eternal sleep, when divine worship was abolished and marriage superseded, the rights of property disregarded and life lavishly and wantonly sacrificed, the atheistical materialism of LaMettrie and von Holbach was seen bearing its appropriate poisonous fruit."[28]

[26]*Op. cit.*, p. 84.
[27]*Op. cit.*, p. 471.
[28]*Op. cit.*, pp. 95 ff.

Flint thinks that the excesses of the French Revolution were logical consequences of French eighteenth century materialistic philosophy. Perhaps it would be more fair to say that materialistic metaphysics in itself, from the abstract philosophical point of view, was just one of the attendant circumstances of the social, economic, political and religious degeneracy of the times.

We have seen that materialism is not necessarily atheistic, neither is it necessarily immoral or amoral. It is fair to say, however, that the God or gods of any materialistic philosophy must be either (1) themselves composed of atoms, in which case they are necessarily finite beings subject to disintegration and decay as the atoms of which they are composed may be separated and scattered; or (2) the God or gods of materialism, if not composed of atoms, are essentially incomprehensible. In this event, it is not denied that individuals may devoutly worship an unknowable and incomprehensible God, but inevitably the unknowable and incomprehensible cannot be the genuine basis of practical moral life. The God of the Judeo-Christian tradition is, of course, far beyond present human comprehension, but is definitely knowable and known as revealed in concrete historical events. Whatever attributes of God may, at present, be unknowable and incomprehensible, at least something is known. In the Judeo-Christian tradition, God's moral law for man as summarized in the Ten Commandments, and God's gracious provision for redemption, are held to be clearly knowable and comprehensible by even the simplest of minds. This Biblical concept of God is entirely impossible for consistent philosophical materialism.

In brief, then, our purpose in including a section on eighteenth century French materialism in this exposition of materialistic philosophy, is not to point to any metaphysical advance or any definite progress made in philosophy, but to gain an historical illustration of a point of view from which materialistic philosophy as such may be evaluated. I believe it is fair to say that it was historically appropriate that the philosophical mind of poor, violently disturbed, eighteenth century France should express itself in materialistic metaphysics.

(7) The Materialism of Feuerbach[29] and Marx

The dialectical materialism of Feuerbach (1804-1872), Marx (1818-1883), Engels (1820-1895) and the modern Marxian socialistic or communistic movement is philosophically interesting as an attempt to combine materialism with the Hegelian dialectic. Hegel (1770-1831) is regarded as an idealist. His theory of logic is called dialectic, a term which will be discussed later in connection with the theory of knowledge. To put the matter in its simplest terms, Hegel believed that all of history moves in successive steps of three stages. First there is the simple situation called "thesis." This is followed by a contradictory situation called "antithesis." The antithesis is resolved into a third stage called "synthesis." The synthesis in turn becomes the thesis for the following triad. Hegel's philosophy as a whole is sometimes called "absolute idealism."

Feuerbach studied for a time as a student under Hegel's philosophical teaching. He later developed his own philosophy as a kind of reversal of Hegel's idealism. Feuerbach was bitterly anti-theistic, and vigorously materialistic. He went to the extreme in his famous saying, *"Der Mensch ist was er isst,"* "Man is what he eats." He retained the dialectic three-stage "logic" of Hegel's system on a materialistic basis. He said that he was turning Hegel's philosophy "right side up," that is, putting materialism in the place of idealism.

Now traditional logic clearly identifies terms, distinguishes them from their contraries, and rejects all contradictories. Dialectic logic (so called) takes the opposite view. "Against the ontology of the separateness and self-identity of each thing, the dialectic laws emphasize the inter-connectedness of all things and self-development of each thing. An A, all parts of which are always becoming non-A may thus be called non-A as well as A. The formula, A is A and cannot become non-A, becomes A is A and also non-A, that is, at or during the same instant . . ."[30]

[29]Feuerbach's *The Essence of Christianity*, George Eliot (tr.) has recently been reprinted (1957) by "Torchlight," Harpers, with introduction by Karl Barth and foreword by H. Richard Niebuhr.
[30]From the article "Dialectical Materialism" in Runes' *Dictionary of Philosophy*. In this article the student will find a convenient and compact discussion of the subject. The bibliography at the end of the article will be useful for those who wish to investigate the subject further.

The uninitiated student will say to himself, how could anyone possibly believe that proposition "A" is both true and false at the same instant? The only answer is that this is Hegelian philosophy, in the idealistic sense, and this is Marxian philosophy, in the materialistic sense. Try to remember your childhood enjoyment of *Alice in Wonderland* and *Alice Through the Looking Glass*. In the latter, "Alice laughed, 'There is no use trying,' she said. 'One *can't* believe impossible things.' 'I dare say you haven't had much practice,' said the Queen. 'When I was your age I always did it for half an hour a day. Why, sometimes I've believed as many as six impossible things before breakfast . . .'" Some philosophers have great enjoyment in believing contradictions, and dialectic thinking keeps them in practice.

Marx and Engels took dialectic materialism from Feuerbach. Thus, as Flint points out, ". . . idealism itself led to materialism. . . . [Hegel] had not been dead eight years before his empire was divided into three conflicting kingdoms, his disciples into three schools, of which one was theistic, another pantheistic, and a third atheistic. In that short period a number of his disciples had found, or fancied that they had found, that absolute idealism was little else than another name for materialism."[31] It should be noted in this connection that David Friedrich Strauss and Bruno Bauer, who had earlier applied Hegelian dialectic to New Testament criticism, were numbered among the young Hegelian materialists.

It is difficult to find in Marx's *Capital* any very clear exposition of the materialistic dialectic, though it is taken for granted in the background throughout. Marx refers to Hegel's *Logic* as an authority.[32] In his Preface to the second edition of *Capital*, which is dated London, January 24, 1873, he makes his philosophical relation to Hegelianism quite clear. He refers to "an excellent Russian translation of *Das Kapital* . . . in the spring of 1872," and to a favorable review in the *European Messenger* of St. Petersburg in May of that year. Of this review Marx says, "Whilst the writer pictures what he takes to

[31]Robert Flint, *op. cit.*, p. 104.
[32]Part III, Chapter XI, pp. 337 f. of the Modern Library edition.

be actually my method, in this striking and . . . generous way, what else is he picturing but the dialectic method?"

Marx continues,

My dialectic method is not only different from the Hegelian, but is its direct opposite. To Hegel, the life-process of the human brain, i.e., the process of thinking, which under the name of "the Idea," he even transforms into an independent subject, is the demiurgos of the real world, and the real world is only the external, phenomenal form of "the Idea." With me, on the contrary, the ideal is nothing else than the material world reflected by the human mind, and translated into forms of thought.

The mystifying side of Hegelian dialectic I criticized nearly thirty years ago, at a time when it [Hegelianism] was still the fashion. But just as I was working at the first volume of *Das Kapital* it was the good pleasure of the peevish, arrogant, mediocre *Epigonoi* [literally "born afterwards" a term referring to the successors of Hegel] who now talk large in cultured Germany, to treat Hegel in the same way as the brave Moses Mendelssohn in Lessing's time treated Spinosa, i.e., as a "dead dog." I therefore openly avowed myself the pupil of that mighty thinker, and even here and there, in the chapter on the theory of value, coquetted with the modes of expression peculiar to him. The mystification which dialectic suffers in Hegel's hands, by no means prevents him from being the first to present its general form of working in a comprehensive and conscious manner. With him it is standing on its head. It must be turned right side up again, if you would discover the rational kernel in the mystical shell.

In its mystified form, dialectic became the fashion in Germany, because it seemed to transfigure and to glorify the existing state of things. In its rational form it is a scandal and abomination to bourgeoisdom and its doctrinaire professors, because it includes in its comprehension and affirmative recognition of the existing state of things, at the same time also, the recognition of the negation of that state, of its inevitable breaking up . . . and is in its essence critical and revolutionary.

The contradictions inherent in the movement of capitalist society impress themselves upon the practical bourgeois most strikingly in the changes of the periodic cycle, through which modern industry runs, and whose crowning point is the universal crisis. That crisis is once again approaching, although as yet but in its preliminary stage; and by the universality of its theatre and the intensity of its action it will drum dialectics even into the heads of the mushroom-upstarts of the new, holy, Prusso-German Empire.[33]

[33]*Capital*, Modern Library edition, pp. 24-26.

The student will gain from the foregoing lengthy quotation not only an indication of the philosophical ancestry of the materialistic dialectic, but also something of the fanatical zeal and earnestness of spirit which has made Marx's teachings so influential.

It seems hardly necessary to point out that Marx's reading of history was erroneous. Neither materialistic nor ideological history actually proceeds in accordance with the Hegelian dialectic of thesis, antithesis and synthesis. The materialistic dialectic theory of the process of history does not correspond to the facts any more than the original Hegelian idealistic dialectic did. The facts of history cannot be forced into a dialectical pattern.

For Marx and Engels, the importance of dialectic materialism was not so much in the field of philosophy as in the field of economics. They taught that the first stage of the logical triad of history, the thesis, was in primitive society, which they held to be communistic. The second stage, the antithesis, they regarded as the present stage of the economic history of the world, namely, the conflict between capital and labor. This antithesis, they believed, would inevitably result in a violent revolution which would lead to the third stage, a "classless society" in which communism would prevail.

According to the Marxian economic philosophy, a proletarian revolution was to be brought about by inevitable forces. Wealth was to be concentrated more and more in the hands of the few until finally the laboring class would rise up in a bloody revolution. A brief period of the "dictatorship of the proletariat" would be followed by a classless society in which all human ills and antagonisms would melt away.

It should be recognized that in his remarkably influential book, *Capital*, Marx pointed out real evils which had developed in the process of the industrial revolution and the growth of the factory system. But the fact that Marx described real evils does not mean that he had the remedy in his dialectical materialism, or in his socialistic program. Many of the evils have been eliminated in the essential processes of the free enterprise system, and many more evils can be eliminated, without resort to a proletarian revolution. Whatever opinions one may have, the fact should be clear that the theory of collective bargaining and the program of the better labor unions, with whatever they have been able to accomplish for the welfare of the laborer, are phenomena strictly within the free enterprise economy, and totally inconsistent with any collectivistic program.

Aside from the errors of the dialectic philosophy, there are three important fallacies in the Marxian economics: One, the labor theory of value is rejected by all scientific economists at the present time. It is recognized that not only labor, but also savings and investment, and direction of capital, are entitled to a portion of the reward of industry.

Two, the widespread distribution of capital through the enormous growth of the modern corporation system was entirely unforeseen. Economists inform us that the capital stock of the great corporations at the present time is owned by literally hundreds of thousands of people in all walks of life, many of whom belong to the laboring classes. Labor unions themselves are among the large owners of capital. On the whole, the managers of the great industrial corporations own only about three per cent of the capital invested. It thus becomes evident that Marx's notion that capital would be more and more concentrated in the hands of the few has proved to be entirely erroneous.

Three, the notion that the revolution and the dictatorship of the proletariat would be followed by a permanent classless society in which human ills and antagonisms would disappear is generally seen to be an unrealistic dream. The dictatorship is a hideous reality in Russia, and no classless society has developed.

In general, in contrast with the materialistic economic philosophy *"Der Mensch ist was er isst,"* "Man is what he eats," we may set forth the saying of Jesus, "Man shall not live by bread alone" (Matthew 4:4; cf. Deuteronomy 8:3).

(8) Emergentistic Materialism

In the discussion of causation in Chapter II emergentistic materialism was briefly mentioned. It was indicated there that no philosophy can consistently defend universal causality. On the one hand atheistic materialism of the older type holds to the eternal being of matter and/or force, never having come into existence, and therefore never having had a cause. At the same time theism holds to the eternal being of God, uncaused. On the other hand emergentism denies the universality of causation, not by adhering to some eternal uncaused being, but by adhering to the theory that something comes from nothing, that is, that finite substantive entities come into existence uncaused.

(a) Hook, Nagel and Edel

The emergentistic materialism of a group of naturalists with whom I have had some contact in the Eastern Division of the American Philosophical Association is not as thoroughly elaborated as some other systems of materialism to which attention has been called, but it is historically and philosophically significant. The individuals named in the subheading above were among those who wrote chapters in *Naturalism and the Human Spirit*, referred to above. Subsequent to the publication of that work, I have heard Professors Edel and Hook take a definite materialistic position in papers read before the A. P. A.

I referred above, in another context, to a statement by Professor Abraham Edel, of City College, New York. In a meeting of the Eastern Division of the American Philosophical Association he said, "It may be argued that a meeting of a philosophical association is in itself sufficient evidence of the fallacy of materialism. On the contrary it should be observed that a meeting of a philosophical association is to be taken as evidence that atoms, when arranged in a particular manner, are capable of assembling together and reading philosophical papers to one another."

In an article entitled, "Critique of Naturalism" in the *Journal of Philosophy* for May, 1945, Professor Sheldon of Yale argued that the naturalists were really materialists. To this charge a reply was made by Professors Dewey, Hook and Nagel in an article entitled, "Are Naturalists Materialists?" in the *Journal of Philosophy* for September 13, 1945.[34]

The emergentism of these naturalists does not quite go the length of asserting that space-occupying entities come into existence with no cause whatsoever. Their emergentism is, in part, merely similar to that of the materialistic dialectic[35] which is committed only to the emergence of values through the rearrangement of space-occupying entities.

The formation of water from hydrogen and oxygen is used in defense of this type of emergentism. These naturalists strenuously protest that they are not "reductionists," they do not reduce present situations to "nothing but" past situations any more than water can be said to be "nothing but" hydrogen and oxygen. The qualities of water are not to be found anywhere in the qualities of hydrogen and oxygen. Minds and mental activity emerge from physical situations, it is held, in a manner analogous to that in which the qualities of water emerge from the chemical combination of hydrogen and oxygen.

A phrase frequently repeated, with variations, affirms that "minds are adjectival and adverbial of bodies." Thus we read, "A non-materialist, on this conception, [Sheldon's] is one who regards minds as substances capable of existing independently of spatio-temporal things, but logically incapable of being adjectival or adverbial of such things. A materialist, on the other hand, is one who believes there is no evidence for the existence of minds so described, and who in addition finds insuperable difficulties in supposing that a mind so conceived can enter into causal relations with anything else. If this is indeed the difference between a materialist and one who is not, then the naturalists whom Mr. Sheldon accuses of materialism are glad to find themselves in his company. . . . In any event, the evidence for naturalism so construed is overwhelming."[36]

[34] I need not take time to point out that the opinions expressed are inconsistent with the metaphysics of John Dewey. Professor Dewey in his advanced years seems to have allowed his name to be used in a variety of ways inconsistent with his own philosophy.
[35] See article "Dialectical Materialism" in Runes' *Dictionary of Philosophy*.
[36] *Journal of Philosophy*, Vol. XLII, No. 19, September 13, 1945, pp. 516 f.

The meaning of the words "adjectival" and "adverbial" in the statements of this group of naturalists is quite amazing. The student knows, of course, what the words mean in their normal context. Adjectives and adverbs are words used to express qualities of substantive entities, actions, states or other qualities. Now what could possibly be the meaning of the statement that minds are adjectival or adverbial of space-occupying entities? Minds are not words, neither are they qualities in the usual understanding of the meaning of qualities. Minds, in human discourse, are thinking things, *res cogitans*. The relationship between minds and physical brains has been much discussed, and will be referred to again under the heading of the metaphysics of realistic dualism. Meanwhile, to say that the relationship between minds and space-occupying entities is "adjectival and adverbial" must be regarded as resort to a metaphor which is totally devoid of intelligible meaning.

The doctrine that minds, and their mental activity, are dependent upon physical things, as advanced by these naturalists, is, of course, nothing new. Their materialism in this respect is not different from that of Hobbes. When matter is organized as we find it in a "living" human body, minds occur. The difference between the recent naturalists and Hobbes is not in their materialism, but in their dogmatic anti-theism.

(b) The Emergentism of Fred Hoyle

The materialism of Fred Hoyle, Fellow of St. John's College, Cambridge, is set forth with the arguments of a modern physics teacher reduced as nearly to a popular level as the subject makes possible. Professor Hoyle is frankly conscious of the data of physics which lead to the conclusion that the present material universe is not eternal, but had a beginning in time, measurable billions of years ago. He states the matter frankly in his *Nature of the Universe.* "Perhaps you may think that the whole question of the creation of the Universe could be avoided in some way. But this is not so. To avoid the issue of creation it would be necessary for all the material of the Universe to be infinitely old. And this cannot be for a very practical reason. For if this were so, there could be no hydrogen left in the Universe. As I think I demonstrated when I talked about the insides of the stars, hydrogen is being steadily converted into helium throughout the Universe and this conversion is a one-way process — that is to say, hydrogen cannot be produced in any appreciable quantity through the breakdown of other elements. How comes it then that the Universe consists almost entirely of hydrogen? If matter were infinitely old this would be quite impossible. So we see that the Universe being what it is, the creation issue simply cannot be dodged."[37]

Evidence that the physical universe cannot be infinitely old has been developed from other lines of argument. According to the second law of thermo-dynamics, in all observable physical processes in the universe some energy becomes less available. In popular language, the physicists tell us that the universe is running down. Since it is far from run down at the present time, it must have had a beginning.

Another physical process pointing in the same direction is the radioactivity of material found in the universe. Physicists know the rate of its disintegration. Coupling this knowledge with a study of other processes in the physics of astronomy, physicists have come to a rather definite conclusion as to the age of the material universe.

These data fall perfectly in line with the theistic view. "The things that are seen are temporary."[38] Professor Fred Hoyle flatly rejects the doctrine of theistic creation: ". . . the older theories . . . assume, as I have said before, that the whole of the matter of the Universe was created in one big bang at a particular time in the remote past. On scientific grounds this big bang assumption is much the less palatable of the two. . . . And I think that of all the various possibilities that have been suggested, continuous creation is easily the most satisfactory theory."[39]

On the question of theistic creation, Hoyle continues, "There is a good deal of cosmology in the Bible. My impres-

[37]Harpers, 1950, pp. 124 f.
[38]II Corinthians 4:18.
[39]*Idem.*

sion of it is that it is a remarkable conception, considering the time when it was written. But I think it can hardly be denied that the cosmology of the ancient Hebrews is only the merest daub compared with the sweeping grandeur of the picture revealed by modern science. . . . It seems to me that religion is but a desperate attempt to find an escape from the truly dreadful situation in which we find ourselves."[40]

His theory is that of the continuous creation[41] of hydrogen atoms throughout the universe. This leads to the question, "Where does the created material come from?" He replies, "It does not come from anywhere. Material simply appears — it is created. At one time the various atoms composing the material do not exist, and at a later time they do."[42]

"The new material does not appear in a concentrated form in small localized regions but is spread throughout the whole of space. The average rate of appearance of matter amounts to no more than the creation of one atom in the course of about a year in a volume equal to that of a moderate-sized skyscraper. . . . The total rate for the observable universe [by the observable Universe he means the Universe within the range of the great telescope at Palomar] alone is about a hundred million million million million million tons per second."[43]

Hoyle's theory of emergence is more elaborately stated in *Frontiers of Astronomy*.[44] The three steps of chemical process by which hydrogen is changed into helium are described[45] and, reinforcing his rejection of theism, Hoyle says, "Men have worshipped things more foolish than reactions i, ii, and iii."

Hoyle claims that his theory can be stated in a mathematical formula as a law of physics. He admits, ". . . a theory of the continuous origin of matter must face up to the challenging issue of determining a mathematical law that serves

[40]*Ibid.*, pp. 138 f.
[41]Although Hoyle uses the word "creation," he makes it perfectly clear that he does not mean creation in any acceptable usage of the word. His theory is that of uncaused emergence.
[42]*Ibid.*, p. 123.
[43]*Ibid.*, pp. 125 f.
[44]Harpers, 1955. Now available in the Mentor inexpensive binding.
[45]*Ibid.*, pp. 67 f.

to control the creation of matter. Let it be said at once that no thoroughly satisfactory way of devising such a law has yet been found. . . . For the present . . . the equations . . . are good enough to enable a number of very interesting results to be obtained."[46]

Again and again Hoyle labors to explain the processes of the physical universe as perfectly uniform and continuous. He says, "It seems as if our system of planets, instead of being in any way exceptional, is a thoroughly normal development of a thoroughly normal star."[47]

"In keeping with the general theme of this book, I believe that nothing arbitrary entered the chain of incident that connected the origin of the earth, and of living creatures on earth, with the general march of cosmic events."[48] As if the appearance of hydrogen atoms without a cause were not in itself the most stupendous discontinuity!

In a rather emotional defense of materialism, he argues, "It is fashionable now-a-days to use the appellation 'materialist' in a derogatory sense, largely I suppose because it has become a catchword in a war of political ideology. This apart, the notion that matter is something inert and uninteresting is surely the veriest nonsense. If there is anything more wonderful than matter in the sheer versatility of its behaviour, I have yet to hear tell of it."[49]

Hoyle strenuously labors to clarify his notion of hydrogen atoms originating without a cause. "The steady potentiality for new atoms to appear in space gives space active physical properties. It is no longer an inert something in which matter resides."[50]

This last statement is indeed amazing. If space has "active physical properties" then, by definition, it is no longer space!

There is another effort to resolve his theory into something intelligible. "The present situation is not new. When a neutron changes to a proton by a *beta* process an electron is

[46]*Ibid.*, pp. 282 f.
[47]*Ibid.*, p. 225.
[48]*Ibid.*, p. 94.
[49]*Ibid.*, p. 201.
[50]*Ibid.*, p. 283.

disgorged. The electron originates. It did not exist before the process, after the process it does. Yet no one ever seems to have been worried by the question of where the electron comes from. We say that it originates in accordance with the laws of the *beta* disintegration."[51]

But physicists understand that the *beta* particle or ray or whatever it is, is not a new creation from nothing, but a changed form of matter/force which previously existed in another form.

Hoyle, by this time, has forgotten that space is the cause of continuous emergence. Endeavoring to draw an analogy, he continues, "Matter is capable of exerting several types of influence — or fields as they are usually called. There is the nuclear field that binds together the atomic nucleus. There is the electro-magnetic field that enables atoms to absorb light. There is the gravitational field that holds the stars and galaxies together. And according to the new theory there is also a creation field that causes matter to originate. Matter originates in response to the influence of other matter. It is this latter field that causes the expansion of the Universe."[52] But the known "fields" referred to are measurable and the transformation of energy and/or matter is also measurable. We can only conclude that the effort to draw an analogy between the electro-magnetic field and other such measurable fields on the one hand, and creation on the other, is an act of desperation!

The uniqueness of the physical earth as a home for human life has long been noted by students of the physics of astronomy. F. R. Tennant[53] of Cambridge has presented the matter as an evidence of the plan of the Creator.

Fred Hoyle, as a materialistic atheist, stands "in opposition to this view at every point." He thinks there are about a hundred billion planetary systems in our galaxy, and ". . . it would be somewhat surprising if anything very different had occurred in any of the other planetary systems. . . . Living creatures must, it seems, be rather common in the universe."[54]

[51]*Ibid.*, pp. 302 f.
[52]*Ibid.*, p. 303.
[53]*Philosophical Theology*, Vol. I, Ch. IV.
[54]*Frontiers of Astronomy*, p. 102.

Hoyle's argument does not in any way depend upon newly discovered data. The number of stars like our sun is of the order of a hundred billion. *Assuming a purely naturalistic explanation for everything in our solar system,* it is assumed that the blind forces of nature would produce similar things in other solar systems. By this reasoning, probably there are billions of Fred Hoyles and billions of books of theories of materialistic emergentism.

On the other hand, we prefer to begin, not with a dogmatic anti-supernaturalistic assumption, but with observed facts. We know that intelligent conscious arrangement of materials and forces, to attain particular premeditated results, *does occur.* We really do not think there are billions of Fred Hoyles, nor that his books are produced by cosmic forces in billions of solar systems. Astronomers are totally without evidence for the existence of any other planet capable of sustaining life as our earth does. Until there is evidence, we find it more reasonable to believe that human life on this planet is the result of a particular conscious purpose.

If there are personal, morally responsible, intelligent beings in other planetary systems, well and good. Angels and demons are referred to in the Bible as beings of such an order, outside of the human family. Our theology will not be disturbed in the least if we find that God has still other personal subjects. So far as evidence goes, this earth seems to be the principal proving ground for the spiritual development of finite personal beings.

C. A Summary

The purpose of the presentation of historical systems of materialism in this chapter has not been primarily historical, but rather expository. It has been thought that the student would best understand materialistic philosophy by studying certain significant influential systems of materialism.

It is my impression that materialism is again on the increase and that the individual who would live effectively in the intellectual atmosphere of our times must understand this old, old philosophy. This is particularly true of the Christian who would intelligently reject materialism in favor of the theistic view.

(1) Materialism and Consciousness

Materialism cannot adequately explain the phenomena of the human mind. The theistic writers of the last part of the nineteenth century have not been superseded in the discussion of this point. The reader will still find Charles Hodge, Robert Flint, James Orr and others of that period quite up-to-date in their method of pointing out that the most intricate knowledge of physical and chemical phenomena will by no means lead to the first step in the understanding of consciousness. Even those who deeply sympathize with materialism, such as Lange, and Bertrand Russell (in the latter's introduction to Lange's *History of Materialism*), recognize that materialism has not yet worked out a satisfactory explanation of consciousness. Fred Hoyle regards this as a problem for the future, though he heaps scorn upon those who believe that a non-material soul or mind could exist without a body. He says, "It is true that some Christians claim to imagine an existence without physical connection. If this is so, then Christians must be endowed with a faculty not possessed by others. I would go so far as to suggest that it is impossible to write a half dozen meaningful sentences concerning such an existence that do not involve some reference to the physical world."[55]

Charles Hodge quotes Professor Tyndale in an address delivered August 29, 1868, as follows:

"The passage from the physics of the brain to the corresponding facts of consciousness is unthinkable. Granted that a definite thought and a definite molecular action in the brain occur simultaneously; we do not possess the intellectual organ, nor apparently any rudiment of the organ, which would enable us to pass, by a process of reasoning, from the one phenomenon to the other. They appear together, but we do not know why. Were our minds and senses so expanded, strengthened, and illuminated, as to enable us to see and feel the very molecules of the brain; were we capable of following all their motions, all their grouping, all their electric discharges, if

[55]*Nature of the Universe*, p. 140.

such there be; and were we intimately acquainted with the corresponding states of thought and feeling, we should probably be as far as ever from the solution of the problem. How are these physical processes connected with the facts of consciousness? The chasm between the two classes of phenomena would still remain intellectually impassable. Let the consciousness of love, for example, be associated with a right-handed spiral motion of the molecules of the brain, and the consciousness of hate with a left-handed spiral motion. We should then know when we love that the motion is in one direction, and when we hate that the motion is in the other, but the 'Why?' would still remain unanswered."[56]

All the evidence goes to show that, aside from extended things, the universe also contains thinking beings which cannot be classified as material objects.

(2) Materialism and God

It has been pointed out above that materialism cannot possibly be correlated with the Judeo-Christian idea of God. Materialism is not necessarily atheistic; this has been historically demonstrated. The god of materialism, however, is either incomprehensible, and thus unapproachable, or he is made up of spatially extended parts, in which case he is finite. The God of the Bible, "a Spirit, infinite, eternal and unchangeable in His being wisdom, power, holiness, justice, goodness and truth" is inevitably rejected by any form of materialistic philosophy.

(3) The Opposite Extreme

However important it is for Christians to understand and to reject materialism, a warning should be given against the opposite extreme. Those who accept the philosophical concepts of the Bible are weakening their own position if they do not recognize plenty of room for physics, chemistry, biology, astronomy and the entire range of material reality, as created by God. In the chapter on idealism we shall see that the denial of matter is likewise inconsistent with the theistic view.

[56]*Systematic Theology*, Vol. I, pp. 251 f.

Chapter IV

IDEALISM

A. *Definitions*

Idealism is far more difficult to define than materialism. The literature is more voluminous, the history is far more complicated. The movements called by the name idealism have a much greater variety of conflicting opinions than we found in the field of materialism.

(1) Not Axiological Idealism

The word idealism is popularly used to describe an attitude of mind toward values. Educators urge young people to have "high ideals." This merely means, "Be devoted to activities which lead to higher values."

Sometimes idealists, in the valuational sense of the word, are regarded as impractical by persons who take what they call a "realistic" attitude toward life and its problems. The "idealistic" individual is sometimes regarded as having his head in the clouds, and disregarding everyday problems. Probably in the majority of cases, in ordinary popular speech, a combination of high idealism with a balance of practical realism is considered desirable.

It should be made clear at the beginning of this chapter that axiological idealism is not the subject under discussion. We fully recognize the well-established proper usage of the words in this sense, but the idealism of values is not what we are talking about.

(2) Not Epistemological Idealism

Idealism in the theory of knowledge is closely related to the subject of this chapter, but it is not quite the same thing. It is that type of philosophy which argues that nothing but mental phenomena can be known by the mind. Professor Brightman, of Boston, lecturing at New York University, said,

"You have never felt a fire, you have only felt heat; you have never seen a fire, you have only seen dancing lights." This type of idealism will be discussed more fully under the heading of Epistemology in Part III of this textbook.

It may be noted that epistemological idealism may be nothing more than a mere tautology. If it is just a tautology, of course we must admit that we see what we see; we hear what we hear; the experiences of the mind are the experiences of the mind. It must be admitted that what we know is mentally known, but this is merely to say that what we know is what we know, since by definition knowing is a function of mind.

If, however, epistemological idealism is more than a mere tautology, it leads directly into metaphysical idealism.

(a) Monistic Idealism

There is a kind of monistic idealism in which epistomological and metaphysical idealism are identical. For monistic idealists (and for some critical realists as well)[1] the process of knowing is held to be a process of becoming identical with the thing known.

(b) Dualistic Idealism

There are idealists (and of course many realists) whose epistemology is dualistic. They recognize that in the knowing process the knower is *other* than the thing known. For idealists who are not monists, epistemological idealism still leads to metaphysical idealism. It is argued that since what we know is mentally known, therefore what we know must somehow be mental in its essential nature.

(3) Metaphysical Idealism

The chief subject of this chapter is that form of idealism which holds that ideas, or spirit, or mental phenomena, are the only things which exist, or which have reality as substantive entities. Referring back to our chapter on the categories, metaphysical idealism holds that the only kind of substantive entity is *res cogitans*. As soon, however, as this has been said,

---

[1]See for example the position taken by D. C. Macintosh in his *Problem of Religious Knowledge*.

objection will be raised. The idealists protest, "Of course we believe in *res extensa!*" But it turns out that for the idealist the extension of what we call material things is only a mental kind of extension. We would define extended things as things which occupy space *regardless of the question of their being perceived in any mind,* and this is what the idealists deny. Metaphysical idealism is the view that everything which exists is in itself ideal, i.e., mind or spirit or thought.

(4) No Degrees of Reality

Reality was discussed in Chapter II under the category of being. It was there suggested that reality, or being, or existence, or the same thought designated by a variety of terms, is a category of other categories. Even a dream may be called real, as when one says, "It was a real dream; I did not make it up."

Usually, however, when the word reality is used the meaning is "real as a substantive entity." I should strongly defend the thesis that in this sense of the word there are no degrees of reality. That which is real is real and that which is not real is not real. Judas is just as real as Simon Peter; a grain of sand is just as real as a human soul. On the contrary it is characteristic of systems of idealism, and I do not know of any exception, to speak in terms of degrees of reality. Reality is more or less confused with value, and that which has the greatest value is said to be the most real.

Accordingly, the definition of idealism in the unabridged *Second Edition* of *Webster's Dictionary* begins as follows: "1. *Philos.* Theory which affirms that mind, or the spiritual and ideal, is of central importance in reality. Specif.: a theory which regards reality as essentially spiritual or the embodiment of mind or reason. . . ."

Note that "of central importance" and "essentially" are value terms, and obscure the question of literal reality.

The definition continues to make the distinction between idealism "which merely affirms the dominance of the ideal element in reality" and idealism "which asserts that the intrinsic nature and essence of reality is consciousness or reason."

I imagine that this definition was composed by idealists.

I do not know of any materialist or dualistic realist who would not agree that "mind . . . is of central importance in reality" or who would deny "the dominance of the ideal element in reality." The words "intrinsic nature and essence" would not be ambiguous if they were accompanied by the statement that ontological idealism denies any reality which does not depend for its being on being known. As the words stand they may well be taken for value terms.

This is not to say that I object to the definition above referred to. A similar ambiguous definition is found in Baldwin's *Dictionary of Philosophy*, Vol. I, p. 500, "In metaphysics: any theory which maintains the Universe to be throughout the work or the embodiment of reason or mind." Let the idealists define their own terms. But I would call attention to the fact that the basic confusion between the concept of reality and the concept of value characteristically makes idealistic discussion of metaphysical reality ambiguous.

The notion of degrees of reality, confused with the notion of degrees of value, is found sometimes in the writings of those who are not idealists. Augustine in his treatise *On Christian Doctrine* says, "For it is because He is good we exist; and so far as we truly exist we are good. And further, because He is also just, we cannot without impunity be evil; and so far as we are evil, so far is our existence less complete. Now He is the first and supreme existence, Who is altogether unchangeable, and Who could say in the fullest sense of the words, 'I am that I am,' and 'Thou shalt say to them, I am hath sent me unto you'; so that all other things that exist both owe their existence entirely to Him, and are good only so far as He has given it to them to be so."[2]

This doctrine of Augustine's, that "so far as we truly exist we are good," is doubtless derived in part from Plato, but it was developed in Augustine's controversies with the Manichæans. It was his reaction against the teaching of Manes that sin is a physical substance.[3]

[2]Book I, Chapter 32.
[3]Augustine's philosophical doctrine that sin is a "privation of being," is discussed by Charles Hodge in his *Systematic Theology*, Vol. II, pp. 157-164. Privation of being is one of Augustine's inconsistencies. He also teaches definitely that sin is positive guilt and corruption.

Thomas Aquinas cannot be properly classed as an idealist, but he quotes Augustine as saying, "inasmuch as we exist we are good," and he argues at length, inconsistently,[4] on the assumption that goodness and being are identical in their various degrees. He identifies *ens perfectissimum*, "most perfect being," with *ens realissimum*, "most real being."

If the student will focus sharp attention on the distinction between reality as a substantive entity on the one hand, and value on the other hand, it will become clear that though there are many degrees of value,[5] there can be no degrees of reality in the category of substantive entity.

(5) Realism, Medieval and Modern

What was called "realism" in medieval times is now a form of "idealism." Inasmuch as the argument between metaphysical idealism and its opponents is an argument as to the nature of reality, the word "real" has been tossed about in a most contradictory manner. In medieval philosophy realism was the term used to designate the type of idealism chiefly derived from Plato's philosophy. "The ideal is the real," was the doctrine in a nutshell. Ideals were believed to correspond to terms designating classes or groups. Such terms were called "universals." Platonists held that the universals, or ideals, preceded the particular things. This doctrine was expressed in the Latin formula *universalia ante rem*, "the universal precedes the particular thing."

Opposed to medieval idealistic realism there arose the philosophy called nominalism, which held that the universal term, or the class name designating the idea of the group or class, is merely a name for the particular things included in the class. The Latin formula for nominalism was *universalia post rem*, "the class name comes after the particular thing."

Modern realism is neither idealism (medieval realism) nor nominalism. Realism in modern usage generally designates that type of philosophy which holds that the universal, or the class name, is not merely a name, neither does it logically pre-

[4]*Summa Theologica*, Book I, question V. See questions IV-VIII and XLVIII-XLIX.
[5]And many kinds of value as well.

cede the particular things which the class name designates, but the reality of the class is found in the reality of the particular members of the class, the class as such being as real as the particulars. The Latin formula is *universalia in re,* "the reality of the universal is in the particular." The reality of the class name is thus held to be in the particular things which make up the class. Modern realism is sometimes erroneously identified with materialism.[6] Those called realists in modern terminology hold to the real existence of extended things, as individuals, and as classes, in the sense that their existence is not dependent upon their being perceived by any mind. But modern realists hold just as firmly to the reality of minds or spiritual beings.

B. *The Idealism of Berkeley*

The historical systems of idealism are so numerous and so divergent that it will not be practical to attempt a survey in chronological order. All that can be done is to sample certain outstanding systems. I have begun with Berkeley because his system of idealism is relatively simple and easy to apprehend.

George Berkeley (1685-1753) spent his scholarly and religious life within the horizons of the Anglican Church. He served as Bishop of Cloyne, Ireland, for almost twenty years, from 1734 until his retirement in 1752 and death in 1753. His chief philosophical work, *Principles of Human Knowledge,*[7] was published in 1710 when he was twenty-five years of age and was serving as tutor in Trinity College, Dublin.

Berkeley should not be regarded as an ivory tower philosopher. He had a keen desire to spread the Gospel among the North American Indians and to raise the standards of the British colonists. To this end he strenuously endeavored to establish a college in Bermuda. He spent nearly three years

[6]The erroneous identification of modern realism with materialism is a persistent error of some of the idealists. See for example *Philosophy of Education* by Rupert C. Lodge. Revised edition 1947, Harpers. See especially the several sections on "realism."

[7]This is reprinted without abridgment in *The English Philosopher From Bacon to Mill,* Edwin A. Burtt, (ed.) The Modern Library, Random House, 1939.

in Newport, Rhode Island, waiting for the promised funds, which never came, for the establishment of his proposed missionary college. In Newport he officiated at Trinity Church. Aside from his missionary interests, following the bursting of the "South Sea bubble,"[8] he wrote an essay in 1721 in political economy on *Preventing the Ruin of Great Britain.*

Berkeley's idealism is summed up in the phrase *esse est percipi,* "to be is to be perceived." In my opinion, Berkeley's is the form of idealism most consistent, most easily understood, and most obviously to be rejected. In a word, he carried epistemological idealism directly into the field of ontology. Since we know only what we know, that is, we know only mentally, therefore nothing exists but mental objects.

The fact that the objects of human knowledge continue even during the periods of time when human beings are not directly thinking of them, and that such objects are available again when human attention is directed toward them, is explained by Berkeley by the simple fact that God continues to think about these objects even when human beings do not. At eleven p.m. I turn out the lights, leave my study and retire for the night. In the morning my desk and my books are just where I left them the night before. They seem to have persisted in their being during the hours when no one paid any attention to them. Berkeley's answer is that God kept all these items in His thoughts during the night, so that they did not cease to exist!

Berkeley's reasons for his idealistic opinions are easily traced in his *Principles.* It is well known that Berkeley was strongly influenced by the philosophy of John Locke, especially by Locke's *Essay Concerning Human Understanding.* He quotes Locke in his introduction[9] to the effect that ability to form general abstract ideas distinguishes man from the beast. Berkeley comes to the opposite conclusion and rejects all general abstract ideas. Quite contrary to the tendency of modern linguistic analysis, Berkeley seeks to clear his ideas of all lin-

[8]An enormous speculative financial hoax, the collapse of which brought on a panic in the business world.
[9]Paragraph 11.

guistic attachments. He says, "He that knows he has no other than particular ideas, will not puzzle himself in vain to find out and conceive the abstract idea annexed to any name. . . . we need only draw the curtain of words, to behold the fairest tree of knowledge, whose fruit is excellent and within the reach of our hands."[10]

In the body of his thesis he argues, "There was an odor, that is, it was smelt; there was a sound, that is, it was heard; a color or figure, and it was perceived by sight or touch. This is all that I can understand by these and the like expressions. For as to what is said of the absolute existence of unthinking things without any relation to their being perceived, that seems perfectly unintelligible. Their *esse* is *percipi*, nor is it possible they should have any existence out of the minds or thinking things which perceive them."[11]

He continues in the next paragraph, "For what are the forementioned objects but the things we perceive by sense? And what do we perceive *besides our own ideas or sensations?* And is it not plainly repugnant that any one of these, or any combination of them, should exist unperceived?" In paragraph 7 he argues, "From what has been said it follows that there is not any other substance than *spirit* or that which perceives spirit. . . . for an idea to exist in an unperceiving thing is a manifest contradiction . . . that therefore wherein color, figure, and the like qualities exist must perceive them; hence it is clear there can be no unthinking substance or *substratum* of those ideas."

In reply to the question *where* matter could exist, he argues, "that it exists not in the mind is agreed; and that it exists not in place is no less certain — since all place or extension exists only in the mind, as has been already proved. It remains therefore that it exists nowhere at all."[12]

He argues that if idolators would only realize that "the sun, moon, and stars, and every other object of their senses" are only "so many sensations in their minds, which have no other existence but barely being perceived, doubtless they

[10]Introduction, paragraph 24.
[11]*Principles of Human Knowledge*, paragraph 3.
[12]Paragraph 67.

would never fall down and worship their own *ideas*, but rather address their homage to that Eternal, Invisible, Mind which produces and sustains all things."[13]

After extended argument Berkeley says, "I think we may lay down the following conclusions. First, it is plain philosophers amuse themselves in vain, when they inquire for any natural efficient cause, distinct from *mind* or *spirit*. Secondly, considering the whole creation is the workmanship of a *wise and good Agent*, it should seem to become philosophers to employ their thoughts . . . about the final causes of things. . . ."[14] As for the general explanation of things ". . . nothing can be more evident . . . [than] the existence of God, or a Spirit who is intimately present to our minds, producing in them all that variety of ideas or sensations which continually affect us, on whom we have an absolute and entire dependence, in short 'in whom we live, and move, and have our being.' "[15]

This knowledge of God is, indeed, not "direct and immediate" but we infer the existence of God as we infer the existence of other persons. "All the difference is that, whereas some one finite and narrow assemblage of ideas denotes a particular human mind, whithersoever we direct our view, we do at all times and in all places receive manifest tokens of the Divinity: everything we see, hear, feel, or any wise perceive by sense being a sign or effect of the power of God. . . ."[16]

With reference to our knowledge of other persons, Berkeley concedes, "From what hath been said, it is plain that we cannot know the existence of other spirits otherwise than by their operations, or the ideas by them excited in us . . . the knowledge I have of other spirits is not immediate, as is the knowledge of my ideas; but depending on the intervention of ideas, by me referred to agents or spirits distinct from myself, as effects or concomitant signs."[17]

It has been observed by others, and it seems apparent to me, that all Berkeley's arguments against the existence of mate-

[13]Paragraph 94.
[14]Paragraph 107.
[15]Paragraph 149.
[16]Paragraph 148.
[17]Paragraph 145.

rial objects, could be employed against the existence of other persons, including God. The result would be what is historically called "solipsism," or the doctrine that no one exists, and nothing exists, but myself.

On the other hand, if it is reasonable for me to infer the existence of other persons by the effects they produce upon my consciousness, or by their actions as their actions are reflected in my perceptions — if it is reasonable to infer the existence of God from the effects which I observe in nature and in personal and social experience, then it is also reasonable to infer the existence of God's *material* creation by its effects as observed in my perceptions.

Berkeley did not intend to deny what the Bible teaches about creation. It should be clear, however, to the careful reader of the Scriptures that the writers thereof always considered the objective creation as something other than God's mere thoughts. It has been consistently held in the Judeo-Christian tradition down through the centuries that God's purposes, His thoughts, His intentions, are from eternity, but that His particular actions in the objective world, especially in His historical deeds in carrying out His plan of redemption, are concerned with space occupying entities which are quite other than mere mental phenomena.

C. *The Idealism of Plato*[18]

Unlike Berkeley's system, Plato's idealism did not grow out of subjective experience; it was not a development of epistemological idealism. Plato's idealism developed definitely out of a search for supreme value. Examining many kinds of virtue led to the conclusion that there is one supreme good which is the arch-type or pattern of all particular goods. All individual virtues are good insofar as they participate in the ideal good. This process of thought led to the notion that for all classes of particular things in the world there are ideas or arch-types or patterns from which the characters of the individuals are derived. These ideas are the realities, and the par-

[18]About 427-347 B.C.

ticular examples are only the shadows. The realities, the ideas, constitute a hierarchy, in which the ideal good, impersonally identified as god, is the supreme reality.

Book VII of Plato's *Republic* sets forth Plato's views in a striking way. The ordinary non-philosophical people of the world are like prisoners in a den or cave, chained in such a position that they are compelled always to face the back wall of the cave. Behind them the cave is open all along the side toward the sunlight. Back of the prisoners, between them and the light, there is a low wall on which people walk back and forth carrying many kinds of objects. The prisoners, never having been allowed to see anything but the back wall of the cave, see only the shadows of the people and the objects. They hear voices, as the shadows move, and they imagine that the voices come from the shadows. So far as they are concerned the shadows are regarded as realities.

It is the function of philosophy to release the prisoners and allow them, or even compel them, to look toward the light and to recognize that what they have regarded as realities are only shadows of the things which are real.

In the illustration of the cave, or the "den" as it is called, the people and the objects which make the shadows are the ideas. These are the realities, according to Plato's view. The shadows on the back wall of the cave represent the particular objects with which individuals ordinarily deal, and which we normally regard as realities.

In the last book of the *Republic*[19] Plato approaches the question of reality, and imitation, from another point of view. He is in the process of condemning certain types of poetry as consisting only of imitation. He argues that although there are many chairs there must be, back of them, as the ultimately real, the ideal chair. Though there are many beds, there must be, back of them, the ideal bed. Particular chairs and beds are imitations of the real. They may be partly real only insofar as they participate in the ideal. They are not perfect, but the ideal chair and the ideal bed are perfect and are really real.

[19]*Republic,* Book Ten, Sections 596 ff.

In these, the particulars, which are not so real, "participate."
Particular things are real only insofar as they participate in
their respective ideas.

In section 247 of the *Phaedrus,* Plato describes, in erotic
terms, a vision of the ideas. As the gods, on the occasion of a
banquet or festival, "move up the steep to the top of the vault
of heaven . . . There abides the very being with which true
knowledge is concerned; the colorless, formless, intangible
essence, visible only to mind, the pilot of the soul. The divine
intelligence, being nurtured upon mind and pure knowledge,
and the intelligence of every soul which is capable of receiving
the food proper to it, rejoices at beholding reality, and once
more gazing upon truth, is replenished and made glad. . . .
[Intelligence] beholds justice, and temperance, and knowledge
absolute, not in the form of generation or of relation, which
men call existence, but knowledge absolute in existence absolute; and beholding the other true existences in like manner,
and feasting upon them, she passes down into the interior of
the heavens and returns home. . . ."[20]

Again in the banquet described in the *Symposium,* Plato
presents Socrates as explaining the true essence of beauty.[21]
He who has been properly instructed, "who has learned to see
the beautiful in due order and succession, when he comes
toward the end will suddenly perceive a nature of wondrous
beauty . . . the final cause of all our former toils . . . everlasting, not growing and decaying or waxing and waning . . . [not
in any particular feature or aspect] but beauty absolute, separate, simple, and everlasting, which without diminution and
without increase, or any change, is imparted to the ever growing and perishing beauties of all other things. He who from
these [growing and perishing beauties] ascending under the
influence of true love, begins to perceive that beauty, is not
far from the end. And the true order of going . . . is to begin
from the beauties of earth and mount upwards for the sake of
that other beauty, using these as steps only, and from one

[20]Plato's *Phaedrus,* Section 247, Jowett translation.
[21]Plato's *Symposium,* Section 211.

going on to two, and from two to all fair forms, and from fair forms to fair practices, and from fair practices to fair notions, until from fair notions he arrives at the notion of absolute beauty, and at last knows what the essence of beauty is."

In other words in ascending from one beautiful thing to another, in which beauty is only partly real, Plato held that one might ascend to the ideal beauty which is really real.

Think of any particular man, and ask yourself, "Is he *really* a man?" Forget that you have changed the meaning of the word "really" to a valuational concept. You may say, "Well, as a man he has some defects." Then proceed to think of a man who is free from these defects and ask yourself, "Is he a *real* man?" Reply, "Yes, but still there are some things about him which might be improved." Then think of the best man you have ever heard of or imagined, and say to yourself, "He *really* is a man!" By this process one may be led step by step to the thought of the ideal man who is the only man who is really real. Other men have the quality of being "real men" only in such degree as they participate in the qualities of the ideal man.

Of course, if we had not shifted the meaning of "real" from the literal meaning to the valuational meaning, we should be clear that all the men in the series are equally real; there are no degrees of reality, though of course there are degrees of approximation to perfection.

The so-called "ontological argument" for the existence of God, presented by Anselm of Canterbury (1033-1109) is entirely dependent upon the Platonic doctrine of the reality of ideas. Anselm argues that since we have in our minds the idea of a Perfect Being, and the idea of a Perfect Being includes the idea of existence, therefore the Perfect Being exists. This argument would have no weight at all unless one believed in the Platonic doctrine that ideas are real. According to the notion of degrees of reality and the reality of ideas, the Most Real Being of all beings would be the Perfect Being.[22]

From the point of view of one who rejects Platonic ideal-

---

[22]Anselm was a great Christian. His *Cur Deus Homo* is a valuable defense of the Biblical doctrine of the atonement.

ism, the Anselmic form of the ontological argument has no weight whatever.[23] It should be apparent that Platonic idealism as a system of ontology cannot be accepted by one who sees that there cannot literally be degrees of reality.

D. *Personalistic Idealism*

Within the nominally Christian horizon the most influential form of idealism for the past half century has been the personalism of Borden Parker Bowne (1847-1910). Bowne taught at Boston University from 1876 until his death. That institution is still the chief center of personalistic philosophy, although personalistic philosophers have held important positions on the faculties of other universities such as Northwestern and Southern California. Bowne said of himself, "It is hard to classify me with accuracy. I am a theistic idealist, a *Personalist*, a transcendental empiricist, an idealistic realist, and a realistic idealist; but all these phrases need to be interpreted. They cannot well be made out from the dictionary. Neither can I well be called a disciple of anyone. I largely agree with Lotze, but I transcend him. I hold half of Kant's system, but sharply dissent from the rest. There is a strong smack of Berkeley's philosophy, with a complete rejection of his theory of knowledge. I am a *Personalist*, the first of the clan in any thorough-going sense."[24] Hocking said of Bowne, "It is the unequivocal insistence upon the attribute of personality in all that is real which marks Bowne off from most of his idealistic colleagues."[25]

Bowne was known as a conservative evangelical in the Methodist Church. He taught both theology and philosophy. I have been told by those who knew him that he was accustomed to preaching in a rescue mission, giving the invitation

[23]Descartes presents a form of the ontological argument as an argument from effect to cause. He held that since the idea of God, as the Perfect Being described in the Bible, cannot be accounted for by naturalistic experiences, this idea must be caused by the actual existence of such a supernatural Being. I have discussed the ontological argument at length in my *Philosophies of F. R. Tennant and John Dewey*, Philosophical Library, 1950. See index.
[24]Quoted by Dean Albert C. Knudson, *The Philosophy of Personalism*, 1949, p. 16. Knudson took the quotation from "A letter dated May 31, 1909, and printed in *The Personalist*, 1921, p. 10."
[25]Quoted by Knudson, *Idem.*

as an evangelist would do, and praying and personally dealing with those who came forward.

My first deep plunge into the literature of idealistic philosophy was in the writings of Borden Parker Bowne. As a student of sociology and theology I had never read much in the field of personalism until, in 1926, I was called upon to teach the courses in Ethics and Theism at Wheaton, where Bowne's textbooks had been used. I dived in and read, as thoroughly and as rapidly as possible, Bowne's five major books, *Personalism, Metaphysics, Theory of Thought and Knowledge, Ethics,* and *Theism.* In the years since then I have read the principal books of Bowne's successors, Brightman and Knudson. I have sought also to make myself familiar with the ideas of Peter Bertocci, a successor of Brightman. The personalists generally profess the Christian faith. I deeply appreciate the earnest spirit and zeal manifested in the writings of those with whom I have had the privilege of acquaintance. In such meetings of the American Philosophical Association as I have been able to attend, I have usually met with the personalists, having more in common with them than with any other group. Nevertheless, I must report that I cannot in any way accept or recommend the personalistic philosophy.[26]

The distinctive feature of personalism, as indicated by Hocking, is "the unequivocal insistence upon the attribute of personality in all that is real." The supreme Person is of course held to be God, and "God is all." Bowne was strong in his denunciation of pantheism, and personalists generally adhere to his opposition. One of the familiar sayings among them is that whereas God is all, yet all is not God. This means, I think, that beginning with the idea of God, everything which exists is within the being of God, as the universal Spirit, the

[26]At a philosophical conference at Manhattan College, New York, Mrs. Ward, wife of publisher, Ward, of Shedd and Ward, told a humorous story to illustrate the differences between Franciscans and Dominicans. A certain Franciscan claimed that he had had a communication from St. Thomas Aquinas in heaven. The Franciscan had asked two questions, "How is it with your theology?" and "How is it with your philosophy?" In answer to the first, Thomas had replied, *"Totaliter similiter,"* "entirely similar." To the second question he had replied, *"Totaliter aliter,"* "entirely different." In spite of friendships, my reaction to personalism is *totaliter aliter.*

"ground" of all that is. But on the other hand, personalism attempts to defend itself against the charge of pantheism by saying, "All is not God." This means, I think, that beginning with observed data in the universe, without the prior assumption that God is all, the observation of the "all" is not identical with a knowledge of God. In other words, personalism rejects the naturalistic approach which says that nature, naturalistically observed, is the only God there is, but personalism insists upon a radically different interpretation of "nature." Nature is not what it seems to the naturalist, but, starting with God, nature is within the being of God. Though not admitted, this, to me, is pantheism.

Bowne, and the idealists rather generally, adhere to the doctrine of personal immortality. Individual persons are believed to have their own created numerical identity distinct from the numerical identity of God. Personal beings, like all other things, nevertheless exist as personal within the being of God. They are real, but not as real as God is.

Bowne thought he could defend the Biblical doctrine of sin and atonement. He held that sin is "real." Yet he taught that sin is not as real as the good. In all of this scheme of things it is apparent that the notion of degrees of reality is fundamental.

It does not seem to me that personalism differs essentially from the theories of Berkeley (discussed above) except in that it insists that the ontological being of everything is not merely thought, but personality, or spirit.

Some of the personalists, like Knudson, hold that God is personal and omnipotent, and some, like the late Herman H. Horne, while clinging to the idea that God is personal, approach the concept of the Hegelian Absolute, identifying God as "the Universal Mind." In an article entitled, "An Idealistic Philosophy of Education,"[27] the relationship between God, called the "absolute mind,"[28] and human personality is expressed by Horne in the sentence, "There must exist a reser-

[27]Forty-first Yearbook of the National Society for the Study of Education, Part One, *Philosophies of Education,* pp. 139 ff.
[28]*Op. cit.,* p. 193.

voir of universal mind before any streamlets of mind can trickle through matter."[29]

On the other hand, an influential group of personalists, following the late Prof. Brightman and Dr. Peter Bertocci, advocate the idea that God is finite in power. Like John Stuart Mill, H. G. Wells, and others, they prefer to deny God's omnipotence rather than to accept the fact that we do not understand the reason for all the evils in the world.

From the point of view of simple Bible-believing Christianity, the notion that God is not omnipotent is blasphemous, and to be rejected with a short, sharp rebuke. This of course is correct, in the circle of those who know the Lord. Perhaps, however, a lesson in the understanding of people with whose ideas we are in sharp disagreement, may not be out of order in this context. I remember well a certain meeting of the Eastern Division of the American Philosophical Association.[30] Dr. Peter Bertocci had given a paper arguing for faith in a personal God. The reaction was bitter and sarcastic. The philosophy teachers in the conference room (perhaps fifty were present) made me think of a snarling pack. Figuratively, it seemed that Bertocci would be torn to pieces. I remember how Sidney Hook said sharply, but earnestly, "Maybe there's a God; maybe there's a fairy on the other side of that lampshade, but I have seen no evidence!" Brightman arose and with deep earnestness, almost with tears, pled with the philosophers, "You ought to believe in God. Don't blame God for the evil in the world. He cannot help it! You ought to enlist on His side and help!"

I wanted to shout, with Isaiah, "Oh that thou wouldst rend the heavens, that thou wouldest come down, that the mountains might flow down at thy presence, . . . to make thy name known to thine adversaries, that the nations may tremble at thy presence!"[31]

I cannot refrain from pointing a moral. We rightly admire missionaries who cut their way through tropical jungles

[29]Op. cit., p. 144.
[30]This was before I became a member and therefore at a time when I did not have a right to speak from the floor.
[31]Isaiah 64:1, 2.

to bring the Gospel to idolaters who are in the condition of darkness described by Paul, "That they should seek the Lord, if haply they might feel after him, and find him, though he be not far from every one of us."[32]

But these words of Paul's were addressed to the Areopagus, that is, the Athenian Philosophical Association. The members were Epicureans and Stoics. Paul had to explain to them that "God that made the world and all things therein, seeing that he is Lord of heaven and earth, dwelleth not in temples made with hands; neither is he worshipped with men's hands, as though he needed anything, seeing he giveth to all life, and breath, and all things."[33]

My point is that the philosophical jungles of our day are just as dense and just as dark as any to be found in tropical Africa or South America. The worshipers of "an unknown God" are just as entitled to a presentation of the Gospel in terms of their language as are those we commonly call heathen. The student of philosophy must understand that the jungles through which he must penetrate, if he is to be faithful to his commission in our so-called civilized areas, are just as difficult as any jungles ever penetrated by Livingstone.

On the doctrine of a finite God, I once said to Dr. Brightman, "I am a Calvinist." His reply was almost a groan! "One reason I believe God is not omnipotent is that evolution took *so long!*" He went into detail as to the long ages when the dinosaurs had to live and die, when the great quantities of oil had to be stored up by the decaying fish (according to a theory) and when things seemed to be moving very slowly.

"You are arguing in a circle," I said. "If God were limited in His power, He might be criticized for delay. But *if God is omnipotent,* the question of how much time He takes is *totally irrelevant.*" He replied that this thought had not occurred to him!

In correspondence I once asked Dr. Brightman how he could eat a sandwich without feeling like a cannibal, if the

[32]Acts 17:27.
[33]Acts 17:24, 25.

115

essential being of everything is personal. His reply was, to me, not at all illuminating.[34]

E. *Absolute Idealism*

The so-called rationalistic absolute idealism of Hegel is too intricate for the compass of the present work and can best be handled in a separate semester's course.[35] Neo-Hegelianism, as exemplified in the teachings[36] of T. H. Green of Oxford, and in the earliest stages of John Dewey's philosophical writings, developed a type of absolute idealism which identified God with the totality of the universe, conceived as the Universal Mind. Although some absolute idealists speak of God as "personal," the God of neo-Hegelianism is hardly to be conceived as a person. Absolute idealism is not necessarily connected with the Hegelian doctrine of thesis, antithesis and synthesis. God is identified as the totality of the cosmic process. God is all, and if there is anything which cannot be included within the being of God, it is relatively, if not totally unreal.[37]

F. *The Idealism of Wilbur Marshall Urban*

Urban is known to many students of philosophy by his article on "Axiology" (the theory of values) in Runes' convenient compilation *Twentieth Century Philosophies*.[38] He is a writer of great weight and what he says is important, whether one agrees with him or not. For a deeper investiga-

[34]The student will find additional valuable information on personalism in Professor Warren C. Young's excellent book, *A Christian Approach to Philosophy*. Professor Young rejects the notion of a finite god and adheres to the Biblical position. His clinging to such phrases as God "the ground" of the universe, and "Cosmic Mind" is, I think, unfortunate, but I believe it is with him a mere verbalism. He definitely rejects the notion that "God is all."

[35]The student will find W. T. Stace's study, *The Philosophy of Hegel*, useful. It was first published in 1923 and is now available in an inexpensive paper back edition by the Dover Publications. For briefer reference, the article on Hegelian Vocabulary by Josiah Royce in Baldwin's *Dictionary of Philosophy* will be found helpful.

[36]I believe H. H. Horne, referred to above, should be classed as a personalist, but his views were near the position of absolute idealism.

[37]Although so-called Christian Science, as a movement in human society, is by no means to be identified with absolute idealism, yet philosophically there are great similarities.

[38]Philosophical Library, 1943.

tion of his type of idealism the student should read *Language and Reality,* the Philosophy of Language and the Principles of Symbolism, Macmillan, 1939, and *Beyond Realism and Idealism,* Allen and Unwin, 1949. Urban's scholarship is of a serious and constructive nature. Though I profoundly and basically disagree, yet I consider the study of his works worthwhile for the fact that he compels the re-examination of the reasons for my Biblical philosophical convictions, if nothing else.

Urban seems to desire to maintain the reality of the *object* of common sense, and to conserve the values of the Christian tradition. Although definitely not a logical positivist (see below), Urban's philosophy is to a large extent a philosophy of language. One peculiarity of his type of idealism is the oft-repeated opinion that language is "constitutive of reality." He holds, quite reasonably, that there is no thought without language, expressed or unexpressed; and that both thought and language are social, in the sense that they necessarily involve communication between individuals, either actual or contemplated.

By "reality" Urban seems to mean the *apprehension* of reality in the mind.[39] In the opinion that language is constitutive of reality, Urban seems to be completely ignoring the notion of truth and reality *as yet undiscovered* by finite minds. To me it seems important to distinguish between *propositional truth,* formulated in the mind, and *ontological truth,* to which, when discovered, propositions ought to *correspond.*

Urban seeks to reassure the realist by saying repeatedly that he believes, just as the realist does, in the reality of substances. He even says, "A natural metaphysics is a substance-attribute metaphysics and traditional philosophy says that, to be intelligible, any metaphysics must be so,"[40] but all this must be understood in the light of the typical idealistic doctrine of degrees of reality, for he concludes, "It may be admitted, I think, without further argument that the category of thing-

[39]Sample instances of the doctrine that language is "constitutive of reality" will be found in *Language and Reality,* pp. 346, 351, 357, 363, 366, 461, 507.
[40]*Language and Reality,* p. 699.

hood does break down when applied literally to the metempirical. Insofar as the notion of substance is identified with this category it breaks down also."[41]

Urban's *Beyond Realism and Idealism,* it seems to me, gets beyond these two views by ruling out realism. He argues, "It cannot be shown, either empirically or logically, that unexperienced entities exist. . . ."[42] He quotes Professor Stace to the effect that "that which is essential to the realistic position is that some entities sometimes exist without being experienced by any finite mind." Urban quotes Professor Stace's reply, "Induction is a generalization from observed facts, but there is not a single case of an unexperienced existence having been observed on which could be based the generalization that entities continue to exist when no one is experiencing them. And there is likewise not a single known instance of the existence of an unexperienced entity which could lead me to have even the slightest reason for supposing that it ever did exist."

Whereas Urban says, "I should not want to put the argument in this extreme form," yet he agrees with Stace in principle. It would seem that for Stace, and for Urban, too, the inside of a peanut does not exist until the peanut is opened![43]

Urban is conscious of the difference between literal logical reality, and degrees of value, but he constantly expresses the hope that value and reality are identical. It does seem to occur to him that, possibly, there could not literally be degrees of reality as such. He frankly refers to "the contradiction between the hierarchical concept of being which arises out of the nature of the good or value, and the apparently non-hierarchical conception which arises out of the notion of logical system. . . . [This contradiction] is also at bottom a conflict between the notion of the categorial supremacy of value, characteristic of *philosophia perennis,*[44] and the categorial supremacy of being."[45]

[41]*Op. cit.,* pp. 699 f.
[42]*Op. cit.,* p. 104.
[43]*Beyond Realism and Idealism,* pp. 108 f.
[44]Perennial (or traditional) philosophy.
[45]*Language and Reality,* p. 726.

With reference to the conflict between the value notion of a "chain of being" leading up to the perfect being, and the logical notion that "to be is to be," and there can be no degrees of being, Urban says, "I should be ready to admit that this apparent contradiction between 'logical system' and the hierarchical conception of being has never been satisfactorily resolved." He seeks to resolve the contradiction by giving a "privileged position" to the notion of the hierarchy of values in being. He concludes, ". . . if any one thing seems to be clear, it is that logical connection is a subordinate notion under the more ultimate criterion of a meaningful whole of experience."[46]

Urban realizes a similar contradiction between the notion of the God of religion and the notion of the Absolute of philosophy. He says, "I suppose that we must admit that the two notions cannot be literally true at the same time. If . . . we recognize that deeper than the demand for absence of logical contradiction is the demand to round out our experience and to make it a meaningful whole, the situation takes on a different character." He repeatedly affirms his belief that *ens perfectissimum* "the most perfect being" is also *ens realissimum,* "the most real being." As indicated in the last quotation above,[47] he is willing to admit logical contradiction in order to round out experience into a meaningful whole.

Urban has much to say about God, but in the end, everything is symbolical and metaphorical, except a few abstractions. "The cosmic myths from which religion gets its language and its symbolism are fundamental elements in every positive religion, and cosmological propositions [are] basal in every religious view of the world. When, as in the Christian creed, it is asserted that God is 'the maker of heaven and earth and of all things visible and invisible,' something of tremendous significance has been said, although it is said symbolically. God, if there be a God, is not a 'maker' in any literal sense. Maker . . . therefore cannot be applied in any empirical or literal sense. In like manner, when in the same creed belief in a 'last judgment' is expressed, something of immense impor-

[46]*Ibid.,* p. 727.
[47]*Language and Reality,* p. 726.

tance has also been said, although symbolically. . . . When these explicit cosmological propositions of religion are interpreted . . . what they are really found to say may be summed up in the statement: *the cosmic significance of values.*"[48]

G. *Other Idealisms and Near-Idealisms*

As indicated at the beginning of this chapter, the systems of idealistic philosophy are so many and so divergent in their nature that a sampling is all that is possible in a work of this kind. However, it is important for the student to realize that there are other systems of idealism besides those which have been described above.

(1) Leibnitz

Leibnitz (1646-1716) is classed as an idealist. His philosophy has been, and still is, of great influence. As a liberal Protestant of the beginning of the period called the *Aufklärung* (enlightenment) Leibnitz took an interest in a futile attempt to bring Protestantism and Roman Catholicism together. Probably his greatest intellectual achievement was the discovery of the differential and integral calculus. His mind was rather technical and mathematical in the theoretical sense. In 1669, when the throne of the Kingdom of Poland was vacant, Leibnitz was asked to write in favor of a German candidate for the crown. This he did, endeavoring to show *by a mathematical demonstration* that it was necessary for Poland to choose a German as its King!

Apparently Leibnitz' idealism did not develop until the more mature years of his life. In his more youthful writings he seemed to regard material things as metaphysically existing. His idealism is developed in his *New Essay,* prepared in answer to Locke. This was ready for publication in 1703-4, but Locke's death prevented Leibnitz from publishing it, and it did not appear until years after Leibnitz' death. With the publication of his *Monadologie* in 1714 his idealism became clearly explicit, though it was never thoroughly systematized.

It was Leibnitz' view that the substance of all things is force, but this force is not physical or mechanical, but rather personal. Leibnitz called it spirit. Force exists in an infinite

[48]*Language and Reality,* p. 619.

number of "monads." These are not atoms, for they occupy no space whatever. They are spiritual entities. They do not interact, but each monad is a mirror, or rather contains a mirror of the universe. Between the monads there is perfect harmony pre-established by God, who is the Supreme Monad and constantly gives off finite monads as emanations from himself. The pre-established harmony is thought of as not purely arbitrary, but produced through the nature of the monads themselves.

Leibnitz was noted for his work in the field of logic. As a mathematician he sought to devise a system of symbolic or mathematical logic. In this he anticipated some of the features of the more modern developments initiated by Boole (1815-1864). Leibnitz' idealism shows distinctively in his enunciation of the "law of sufficient reason" in logic.[49]

It might be safe to say that there is a psychological relationship between Leibnitz' mathematics and his metaphysics and logic. Focusing his mind upon abstract infinitesimal values, he loses connection with the created world of substantive entities and brute facts. His monads are hardly existing beings, but are more like the infinitesimals in calculus.

(2) Phenomenology

The word phenomenology used by Kant and then in a different sense by Hegel, now describes a considerable number of somewhat divergent views. The one thought which seems to run through all types of phenomenology is that only phenomena can be known. Edmund Husserl (1859-1938) is said to have been the first one to apply the name phenomenology to a whole system of philosophy. There is an historical and analytical article on this subject six columns in length in *Runes' Dictionary of Philosophy* which will be valuable for the student who wishes to pursue the subject.[50]

[49]See Chapter I, pp. 23 f.
[50]There is a typographical misplacement of an entire column of this article on p. 233. This can be straightened out by the following procedure: Read column one, p. 233, down to the eighth line from the bottom. From here skip to the top of column two, p. 233. From the end of column two, p. 233, go back to line seven from the bottom of column one. After the last line of column one, p. 233, turn to p. 234. The article is really worth the effort. *Runes' Dictionary of Philosophy* is well printed. This is the only typographical error that I have noted.

Some phenomenologists hold, with Kant, to the metaphysical existence of material substantive entities, of which phenomena are manifestations. Others take a more distinctively idealistic position and regard phenomena as the only metaphysical realities.

(3) Logical Positivism[51]

Positivism is a term brought into prominence by Auguste Comte (1798-1857) in the middle of the nineteenth century. As a philosophy it claimed to be occupied with the simple description of sensory phenomena. Hume (1711-1776) is usually called a positivist, although the name "positivism" did not originate in his period. Logical positivism also goes by the names "scientific empiricism," "unity of science movement," "logical empiricism," and "analytical philosophy." This movement originated in Vienna in the so-called "Vienna circle" in 1924.

Rudolph Carnap (born 1891) was a prominent original member. Carnap went to the University of Chicago in 1936. Hans Reichenbach (1891-1953), who served on the faculty of the University of California in Los Angeles from 1938, was a prominent member of the movement. His book *The Rise of Scientific Philosophy* is frequently referred to by Professor Warren Young in his *Christian Approach to Philosophy*. Professor Young discusses logical positivism at some length.

In his chapter in the Schilpp volume on *The Philosophy of John Dewey*, Reichenbach seeks to show that Dewey is actually a logical positivist. In his reply, Dewey politely declines the honor. The philosophy of Ludwig Wittgenstein (member of the faculty of Cambridge University from 1929 to 1947) had an important influence in the logical positivist movement. His *Tractatus Logico-Philosophicus* published in 1922 strongly influenced the Vienna circle at its beginning.

The logical positivists have been feverishly active in producing literature. There are many divergences and the move-

[51] Daniel Sommer Robinson gives an incisive critique of logical positivism in his chapter entitled, "The Right to Be Wise," Chapter XV, in *Crucial Issues in Philosophy* (Christopher Press, 1955, pp. 137-145). His scholarship and wit are here irresistible. See also general references to logical positivism given in the introduction p. 29.

ment cannot be said to have crystallized with any degree of unanimity. However, on the affirmative side it is characteristic of this group of philosophers to emphasize linguistic analysis and a symbolical mathematical form of language for the expression of scientific material.

Negatively, the entire logical positivistic movement is characterized by antagonism to metaphysics of any kind. It is generally held that such questions as, "Does matter exist?" "Does God exist?" "Is causality real?" "Is free will real?" are not only unanswerable, but totally meaningless. Similarly, ethical judgments are held to be meaningless. All ethical statements such as, "It is wrong to bear false witness against a neighbor," are to be understood as merely emotional expressions, such as, "I don't like a false witness."

(4) The Metaphysics of John Dewey
(1859-1952)

I have written elsewhere[52] at length upon John Dewey's metaphysics. At the beginning of his long career, Dewey held to the neo-Hegelian absolute idealism of T. H. Green (1836-1882), the famous and influential professor of moral philosophy at Oxford. Dewey, in an article entitled, "Soul and Body" in the *Bibliotheca Sacra*, Vol. 43, April 1886, spoke in traditional pious terms in defense of faith in God. It is clear, however, that by the word God he meant the Universal Mind, or the Absolute, not the personal God of the Bible. Dewey wrote his famous article, "The Reflex Arc Concept in Psychology" in 1896. It was about this time that Dewey made the transition from idealism to the type of anti-metaphysical metaphysics which he maintained throughout the remaining years of his long career. He definitely abandoned idealism and strongly attacked the notion of the existence of a substantive mind as a thinker, either human or divine.

[52]*Philosophies of F. R. Tennant and John Dewey*, Philosophical Library, 1950. For an able discussion of "process" philosophy, based largely on Whitehead and Bergson rather than Dewey, but essentially the same as Dewey's view, see "Substance, Process, Being" by A. W. Levi of Washington University, St. Louis, in the *Journal of Philosophy* for August 28, 1958, Vol. LV, No. 18. And for an excellent reply defending "substance" philosophy, i.e., recognizing substantive entities at least in the material realm, see "Substance, Process, and Nature" in the same issue, by Andrew J. Reck of Tulane University.

Dewey never became a materialist and never admitted the existence of material objects prior to the human inquiry process. Perhaps it was his thorough-going anti-supernaturalism which prevented him from adopting a materialistic view. In his *Common Faith*[53] he says, "As long as the conceptions of science were strictly mechanical (mechanical in the sense of assuming separate things acting upon one another purely externally by push and pull), religious apologists had a standing ground in pointing out the difference between man and physical nature." Dewey avoided metaphysics and repeatedly denied the existence of any kind of substantive entities. The only realities recognized by him are events within the social inquiry process.

For years Dewey called his philosophy "pragmatism" but with the publication of his *Logic* in 1938, he said that the word pragmatism had become so ambiguous that he had abandoned it. Although he sometimes used the word pragmatism in his later writings, he thought "instrumentalism," or "experimentalism" (preferably the latter), less ambiguous.

It may be argued that Dewey's metaphysics should not be included in a chapter on idealism. Indeed, it is not idealism, but I would class it as near-idealism. The only reality of which the world is made is the social inquiry process with its events. Both mind and matter are vigorously denied, but the events of this inquiry process are a "stuff" similar to thought.

(5) The Metaphysics of F. R. Tennant
(born 1866)

My more extended work on the philosophy of Tennant is referred to above. Tennant in his early days was an idealist. He gave up idealism and became to all intents and purposes a dualistic realist, but his idealistic forms of thought still clung to him. In the end he considered it likely that the "stuff" of which the universe is made is, after all, spirit, though he continued to recognize the objective reality of material things, whatever they may be made of.

[53]Yale University Press, 1934, p. 54.

(6) Survey

The student who wishes to study a cross-section of the idealistic philosophy of the recent past should read a volume entitled *Contemporary Idealism in America,* published by Macmillan in 1932. It is written by a galaxy of brilliant lights among idealistic philosophers. Professor Barrett of Princeton is the general editor. A dedicatory chapter in memory of Josiah Royce was written by Professor Palmer of Harvard. Other authors are Professors Bakewell of Yale, Hocking of Harvard, Cunningham of Cornell, Urban of Yale, Leighton of Ohio State, Brightman of Boston, Boodin of U.C.L.A., Tsanoff of Rice Institute, Hendel of McGill and Hoernlé of the U. of Witwatersrand, Johannesburg, South Africa. The book is rather a survey than a piece of propaganda for any one idealistic view.

A competent expression of idealism in the recent past is found in *Crucial Issues in Philosophy,* by Daniel Sommer Robinson of the University of Southern California.[54] His chapter "Absolute Idealism Today" advances a kind of neo-platonic mysticism coupled with the Hegelian doctrine of the Absolute Mind. Approximately half of Robinson's book is devoted to a review of the philosophies of prominent idealists in the recent past.

[54]Christopher Publishing House, Boston, 1955.

Chapter V

DUALISTIC REALISM

Recapitulation

Before proceeding with dualistic realism it will be well to draw together, in diagram form,[1] several important types of ontology for purposes of comparison. First of all materialism may be represented by a continuous row of squares, as follows:

□ → □ → □ → □

Materialism refuses to recognize any other substantive entity besides physical matter. Some materialists, like Watsonian behaviorists, ignore or deny consciousness. Others recognize consciousness as an aspect of matter, but none will recognize mind or spirit as a substantive entity.

Idealism may be represented with a continuous row of circles, as follows:

O → O → O → O

Idealism refuses to recognize any kind of substantive entity other than mind or spirit or thought or idea.

Parallelism is a type of ontology which we have not discussed in detail. It may be represented by two continuous rows, one of squares and one of circles, with no connection between them:

O → O → O → O

□ → □ → □ → □

The philosophy of parallelism is exemplified by the writings of George Stuart Fullerton of Columbia University whose *Introduction to Philosophy* was published in 1916. Fullerton recognized the reality of material things in a causal series,

[1]These diagrams are adapted from an article by V. J. McGill in *Science and Society*, Vol. 9, No. 4, Fall of 1945.

and the reality of mental phenomena in a series, but he denied that matter has any effect upon mind or that mind has any effect upon matter.

The philosophy of Leibnitz was parallelistic in another sense, namely that there is no interaction between the monads but that they operate by a pre-established harmony. However, Leibnitz' parallelism is a form of idealism and is not like the parallelism of Fullerton.

A parallelistic ontology like that of Fullerton was taught in certain courses in psychology which I had at Minnesota before Watsonian behaviorism came into popularity.

Epiphenomenalism may be illustrated by the following diagram in which we have a continuous line of circles parallel with a continuous line of squares, with arrows pointing from the squares to the circles but not in the opposition direction.

O – O – O – O
□ – □ – □ – □

This view of ontology was represented by the late George Santayana, who called himself a materialist but recognized the fact of consciousness as running parallel with the material changes of events. It was his opinion that material causes produce mental effects but that the mental chain of events never exerts a causal influence upon material things. The experiences of the mind, then, are not to be taken as experiences of a substantive entity but only as epiphenomena, that is phenomena which are over and above, and not actually a part of reality.

C. D. Broad[2] devotes a considerable amount of discussion to the theory of epiphenomenalism. Broad is cautious about committing himself to any conclusion, but he believes that epiphenomenalism would be the most probable ontology *if* there is no personal immortality. In his final conclusion,

[2]*The Mind and Its Place in Nature,* Harcourt, Brace & Co., 1925.

however, he cautiously advances a theory of progress which makes it necessary to suppose that mind does causally exercise control over matter.

Dualistic realism is represented by the following diagram in which the mental series of events runs parallel to the material series of events, with arrows pointing in both directions, as follows:

$$O - O - O - O$$
$$\nearrow\!\!\!\swarrow \quad \nearrow\!\!\!\swarrow \quad \nearrow\!\!\!\swarrow$$
$$\square - \square - \square - \square$$

It is the belief of dualistic realists that such a diagram represents what actually goes on in the world. There are mental events and there are material events and it is a daily experience that purposes in the mind release energy in the body and produce effects in the material world, just as events in the material world, through the sensory organs, produce events in the mental world.

John Dewey's metaphysics is difficult to represent by a diagram in any way similar to the others. Thus far, the diagrammatic scheme, though greatly over-simplified, does convey an intelligible impression. Dewey, however, as has been explained above, denies substantive entities either of material or of spiritual nature. McGill, in the article referred to above, diagrammed Dewey's metaphysics by a series of circles superimposed upon squares, thus attempting to represent situations which are neither mental nor physical. It seems to me more appropriate to represent Dewey's metaphysics merely by a series of crossed arrows leading from nothing to nothing, as follows:

$$\times \quad \times \quad \times \quad \times \quad \times$$

Dewey's events in the social process are dynamic situations in which nothing very intensely acts upon nothing, which was never there before the event took place. The action continues until a goal is reached, which proves to be, not a goal, but another situation requiring a further resolution, and so on.

A. *Outstanding Exponents of Dualistic Realism*[3]

Dualistic realism is by no means new or uncommon, but every important philosophical conception has to redefine itself in the details of its development, and has to defend itself with reference to the various attacks made upon it, and the various reactions to it, as time goes on. Professor Elias H. Johnson, D.D., of Crozer Theological Seminary, in a series of articles published in the *Examiner* in 1894 and 1895, opposing the idealistic evolutionary pantheism of Augustus Hopkins Strong, describes his own view as dualistic realism.

Charles Hodge, the great theologian of Princeton in the nineteenth century, in his *Systematic Theology,* under the heading, "Realistic Dualism" writes as follows:

> The Scriptural doctrine of the nature of man as a created spirit in vital union with an organized body, consisting, therefore, of two, and only two, distinct elements or substances, matter and mind, is one of great importance. It is intimately connected with some of the most important doctrines of the Bible; with the constitution of the person of Christ, and consequently with the nature of His redeeming work and of His relation to the children of men; with the doctrine of the fall, original sin, and of regeneration; and with the doctrines of a future state and of the resurrection. It is because of this connection, and not because of its interest as a question of psychology, that the true idea of man demands the careful investigation of the theologian.
>
> The doctrine above stated, as the doctrine of the Scriptures and of the Church, is properly designated as realistic dualism. That is, it asserts the existence of two distinct *res,* entities, or substances; the one extended, tangible, and divisible, the object of the senses; the other unextended and indivisible, the thinking, feeling, and willing subject in man. This doctrine stands opposed to materialism and idealism, which although antagonistic systems in other respects, agree in denying any dualism of substance. The one makes

---

[3]Among historical dualistic realists the name of Immanuel Kant is outstanding. He vigorously rejects the charge that he is an idealist. See e.g. Remarks II and III following sections 13 of his *Prolegomena.* However, his view of "things in themselves" is too complicated for illustrative use here.

the mind a function of the body; the other makes the body a form of the mind. But, according to the Scriptures and all sound philosophy, neither is the body . . . a precipitate of the mind, nor is the mind a sublimate of matter.[4]

The article entitled, "Education and the Realistic Outlook" by Professor Frederick S. Breed in *Philosophies of Education*[5] clearly exemplifies dualistic realism, except that Breed does not come out squarely for the ontological reality of the mind or soul as a substantive entity. The chapter by Professor John Wild "Education and Human Society; a Realistic View" in the fifty-fourth Yearbook of N.S.S.E. (1955) supports dualistic realism, and, in a way, supports creationism, though there are many points at which one would disagree.

The volume entitled *The New Realism*[6] containing essays by Holt, Marvin, Montague, Perry, Pitkin and Spaulding indicates a dissatisfaction with idealism, but scarcely gets away from it, and rather definitely avoids dualistic realism. Another volume entitled *Essays in Critical Realism*[7] by Drake, Lovejoy, Pratt, Rogers, Santayana, Sellars and Strong supports the realism of material things, but avoids the reality of the mind or soul and, in some of the essays, even avoids the dualism of subject and object in epistemology. This work purports to be primarily a study in epistemology. ". . . no agreement has been sought except on the epistemological problem with which this volume is concerned; and, actually, the members of our group hold somewhat divergent ontological views." (Preface)

The excellent article on "Epistemology" by Principal James Iverach of Aberdeen, in Hastings' *Encyclopaedia of Religion and Ethics*, Vol. V, pp. 337-356, reflects genuine integrated dualistic realism together with the doctrine of creation.

In general outline, though not in specific detail, dualistic realism is the common sense philosophy of Thomas Reid

[4]*Systematic Theology*, Charles Hodge, Scribners, 1871, Vol. II, p. 46. See also the usage of Prof. Elias H. Johnson of Crozer, a younger contemporary of Charles Hodge, who took the same philosophical viewpoint. Cf. articles on "Realism" and "Dualism" in such works as Baldwin's *Dictionary of Philosophy*.
[5]Forty-first Yearbook of N.S.S.E., 1942.
[6]Macmillan, 1912.
[7]Macmillan, 1920.

(1710-1796) and James McCosh (1811-1894), though there are important differences.[8]

B. *Distinctions*

(1) Not Ethical Dualism

Dualistic realism in ontology is entirely distinct from the form of philosophical dualism which, in the field of ethics, is exemplified by Zoroastrianism. It has been held, especially in non-Christian philosophy, that good and evil are equally eternal. The student will readily recognize that this is not the form of dualism here advocated.

(2) Not Eternal Metaphysical Dualism

Dualistic realism is a convenient term by which those who adhere to the Bible may designate the metaphysical nature of the created world. The term does not imply eternal dualism in ontology. The Bible, and the Bible only, in the entire history of human culture, is the source of the doctrine of creation out of nothing. No other philosophy or religion, except those derived from the Bible, teaches this doctrine. Without exception the philosophies and religions of the world not derived in this respect from the Bible, if they have anything to say about the origin of things, seek to explain the present world order as having arisen from a previous order of previously existing materials. Human culture has many cosmologies but, strictly speaking, only one cosmogony.[9]

The doctrine of creation out of nothing is not only found in the early chapters of Genesis, but it is implied, or explicitly taught, wherever the creation of the world is referred to in the Bible: "By the word of the Lord were the heavens made; and the host of them by the breath of his mouth. . . . For he spake and it was done, he commanded and it stood fast" (Psalm 33:6, 9). In John 1:3 we read: "All things were made by him: and without him was not anything made that was made." It is

[8]The student should understand that "common sense" in Scottish philosophy does not have exactly the same meaning as in popular vernacular. It is not merely "horse sense." It refers to the kind of criterion of truth summarized by Vincent of Lerins (died 450 A.D.), "*quod semper quod ubique quod ab omnibus creditum est*" ("that which is believed always everywhere by all").
[9]"Cosmogony" is based on *kosmos* and the perfect stem of *ginomai, gon (gegona)*. The word means "beginning of the cosmos."

important to note that the word here translated "made" is not the usual word for making out of previously existing materials, *poieo,* but it is the word which means to come to pass, *ginomai.* The verse might properly be translated, "Everything came into being by him and without him not one thing came into being which has come into being."

A still more striking example of the doctrine of creation out of nothing is found in the Greek text of Hebrews 11:3. In the ordinary English translation we read, "Through faith we understand that the worlds were framed by the word of God, so that things which are seen were not made of things which do appear." The word translated "things which are seen," literally, "that which is looked upon," is *blepomenon,* and the word for "things which do appear" is the genitive plural of *phainomenon.* In the statement that "that which is looked upon does not come from things which put in an appearance," we have, I think, a simple statement of the doctrine of creation out of nothing.

The data of the physics of astronomy now corroborate the Biblical doctrine that the material universe is not infinitely old. We do not hold to an eternal dualism of matter and mind, but to an actual, realistic dualism in the present created order of things.

(3) Not Materialism

It would hardly seem necessary to make the statement that dualistic realism is not to be identified as materialism, but there seems to be a tendency, previously mentioned, among certain idealistic writers to accuse all who adhere to realism in the modern sense of the word of being nothing but materialists. It is true that realism in the modern sense of the word indicates the genuine reality of material things, but this does not mean that realists deny the genuine reality of thought or spirit.

(4) Not Aesthetic Realism

In the field of the fine arts, realism is a term frequently used to describe the view which is contrasted with romanticism. The propriety of this aesthetic use of the word is not for a moment questioned.

Aesthetic realism is similar to a type of realism referred to in ordinary discourse describing an attitude of mind other than visionary. To be realistic in this sense, means to be practically minded. It should be quite evident that dualistic realism in the field of metaphysics is not to be confused with realism in the sense of aesthetic realism, or of mere practical mindedness.

(5) Not the Realism of Ideas

The ancient realism of Plato has been discussed above, and it has been made clear that realism in the modern sense of the word is not to be identified with Plato's doctrine of the reality of ideas.

In the history of American theology, Jonathan Edwards (1703-1758) held to a philosophy of idealism closely akin to platonic realism, with its theory of degrees of reality. This doctrine caused confusion in his presentation of the relationship of humanity to Adam in original sin, and to Christ in the atonement.

Although not a thorough-going idealistic "realist" like Jonathan Edwards, the noted theologian William G. T. Shedd (1820-1894) taught a doctrine of generic humanity which was similar to platonic idealism.[10]

(6) Not Parallelism

In my more extended work on the philosophy of John Dewey, referred to above, I have called attention to the fact that he never fairly confronts dualistic realism, but almost without exception assumes that dualistic realism is identical with the philosophical parallelism of his earlier contemporary, Professor Fullerton, whose parallelism is mentioned above on page 126 f. Dualistic realism is a philosophy of the interaction and integration of the really existing material and spiritual substantive entities in the universe.

(7) Not Arbitrary or Exclusive

Dualistic realism does not arbitrarily or exclusively select material things and spiritual beings as though there could not

---

[10]The objections to the "realistic" views of Edwards, Shedd and others are presented by Charles Hodge in his *Systematic Theology*, Vol. II, pp. 51 ff., 54 ff., 61 f., 216, 222, 449, and Vol. III, pp. 200, 652 ff., 656 ff. On the realism of Edwards, see Vol. II, pp. 207 ff., and p. 217.

be any other kind of existences. In the chapter on the categories I have indicated that the word reality may apply to any concept in any of the categories. The name dualistic realism is selected for its convenience and for the importance of the two kinds of things to which the term points. It simply means that within the category of substantive entities we find two important interacting, integrated sub-categories, extended things and spiritual beings or minds. Dualistic realism is not arbitrarily committed to any particular dogma on the nature of material things or the nature of minds except that material things are extended in space and that minds are beings which think.

C. *The Nature of Matter*

Dualistic realism is definitely committed to the doctrine that material things, since the creation of matter, exist in distinguishable numerical identities as substantive entities other than mind or thought. In his definition of realism in Baldwin's *Dictionary of Philosophy* (published in 1902) John Dewey said, "Realism . . . in the more modern . . . theory . . . is the doctrine that reality exists apart from its presentation to, or conception by, consciousness; or that if, as a matter of fact, it has no separate existence to the Divine consciousness, it is not in virtue of anything appertaining to consciousness as such." This comes close to it. Opponents of modern realism frequently describe it as the view that matter is "independent" of mind. They then proceed to argue that all things are dependent upon the mind of God, whether God is conceived as a personal being or a cosmic intelligence. The word "independent" is misleading. Christians certainly believe that all things which do exist, and all their relationships, are dependent upon God and are known by His mind.

(1) The Biblical View

The Biblical position is not that matter has "no separate existence to the Divine consciousness." In affirming the omniscience of God, we do not affirm that being as a substantive entity, and being known, are indistinguishable.[11] We do not

---

[11]Note that the word distinguishable is less ambiguous than Dewey's word "separate."

accept the superficial dogma that for God to know and to do are identical. We do not regard material things as objects of continuous creation. Neither do we regard them as independent of the Divine will. I suggest that in describing the ontological status of material things the words "separate" and "independent" are inappropriate. "Distinguishable" is a more precise term.

Dualistic realists do accept Dewey's words, "Reality exists . . . not by virtue of anything appertaining to consciousness as such," that is, since creation. The Biblical writers uniformly regard the creation of the universe as a *fait accompli,* a process which has been completed.[12] Throughout the writings of the Bible, material entities are regarded, not necessarily as separate, not as independent, but as literally existing in reality as substantive entities in the status of distinguishable numerical identities.

(2) The External Evidence

Dualistic realism accepts the testimony[13] of the senses in a manner similar to that in which testimony is accepted in the wider horizons of human society. We read the newspapers. We listen to the news reports, and we form our own opinions about events in the world near and far. The testimony may be conflicting; our interpretation may be erroneous. Nevertheless, in the large, we gain a considerable amount of information from testimony. We accept that which is integrated, that which does not contradict itself, and that which corresponds to previous or subsequent investigation. In a similar way in our individual horizon we accept the testimony of our senses.

I draw a chair up to a table and proceed to write. For a long time, especially since Eddington's famous Gifford lectures of 1927, the popular mind has been confused about "my two tables," and it might be said with some justification that the teachers of philosophy in our universities have not decreased, but have generally increased the confusion.

Eddington explained that one of his tables is what we

12Genesis 2:1-3, Exodus 20:11, Hebrews 4:4-10.
13Metaphysics and epistemology overlap. This will be more apparent when we come to Part III.

think of as a table in ordinary speech, that is, a piece of furniture with a flat surface suitable for writing. The other table is what the table "really" is in its atomic structure. The atoms are constantly in motion like a swarm of flies. The inter-atomic spaces and intra-atomic spaces are greater in proportion to the solid material than the space within the solar system in proportion to the mass of the sun and the planets macroscopically considered. The ordinary table thus disappears in a weird, unknown, mysterious, scientific thing which is supposed to be "real." I suggest that the answer to this confusion is to increase the number of tables by an indefinite factor. My table is not only a solid surface for writing, but as a cabinet maker I know my table as intricately fashioned pieces of wood with mortices, tenons, pores, grain, glue, varnish, drawers, compartments, and a complicated system of locks. As a homekeeper, my wife knows the table as a locus of dust and finger marks, and sometimes papers and books which appear to be chaotic. As I sit across the room from my table, the surface seems to have two acute angles and two obtuse angles. Reflectively, I think of the table as rectangular, but seldom if ever is the visual image of the table actually rectangular.

Now which of these many tables is "real"? The answer of dualistic realism is that all of these tables, including the ones known to the atomic physicist, are equally real, as aspects of one numerical identity, the table. There is no more reason to regard the table of ordinary uses as unreal after one becomes acquainted with the table of atomic physics, than there is to regard a carpenter as no longer a carpenter after learning that he is also a husband and a father.

Perhaps the strangeness of many aspects of the physical world is a matter of childhood training. At least for myself I must testify that I have grown up with Eddington's two tables as one.[14] As a youngster in the first grade I remember hearing my uncle say to my mother, "Isn't it strange that we don't really see anything, but that what we think we see only gives

[14]Not that the atomic physics of my childhood is identical with that of today, but the presently known intricacies of the atom have not in the slightest degrees modified the essential concept of reality.

off rays of light which strike our eyes?" My mother replied, "It doesn't seem strange to me. That's what we mean by seeing things." Thus from my childhood the physical analysis of the mechanics of the material world by which our sensory organs are affected, has never impressed me as in any way strange. It is a thrill to hear the voices of our daughter and her family by telephone from Tokyo; but the voices by telephone are perfectly real. The mechanical resonance and the "static" are also real. We constantly use the dictaphone, the microphone and television without doubting reality. The many different aspects of physical analysis have never given me the feeling of unreality in any particular viewpoint.

The intellectual problem of knowledge based upon testimony and evidence will be taken up in the discussion of epistemology. In the present discussion, which is ontological rather than epistemological, we are simply indicating what we believe to be real, rather than the process by which we come to such a conclusion.

Briefly then, the material world is accepted as real in a complex but unified sense. As I write in my study I hear through the open window the voices of a bob white, a mocking bird and a cardinal. From previous experience I infer that the living birds are out there in the trees and in the tall grass. I believe that I could observe them from many points of view by the sense of sight as well as hearing. All the testimony being consistent, and there being no contradiction involved, I postulate their reality.

I have just listened to the radio news and heard of assassinations in a distant country. This report integrates with a considerable number of other testimonies in regard to the disorder in that struggling land. The reports may be somewhat contradictory, and the inferences in my own mind as well as inferences drawn by the political reporters and analysts may be partly erroneous. From the testimony, however, I postulate the reality of the situation.

The radio and the newspaper have recently brought a most astonishing report of a submarine trip under the Arctic ice cap to the other side of the world. It is reported that from

Point Barrow there is a valley in the ocean bottom leading to the main basin of the Arctic Ocean, and it is reported that at the North Pole the Arctic Ocean is something over 13,000 feet in depth. Whereas, at the first report, I had a sensation of claustrophobia, when I read the report of the soundings, I began to believe that submarine passage under the Arctic ice cap may well be commercially practicable.

In all these illustrations the one point should be simple and clear, namely that we receive testimony, we combine and examine the evidence, and we postulate physical factors in the outside world as substantive entities. Widen the horizon to the entire social consciousness of man, or narrow the horizon to the individual reflective consciousness, the process is the same in principle: the reasonable postulation of material existences in the world in which we live.

Beyond the postulation of space-occupying substantive entities, we are not philosophically concerned in the nature of matter. For the ordinary purposes of a professor of philosophy or a minister of the Gospel, atomic chemistry and physics are not immediately important. I can leave the details to the specialists. But these fields are intensely interesting. We desire to know more, not for philosophical or theological reasons, but because we are naturally interested in the world around us. As Christians we are interested in the nature of the created world.

I have heard a theory of the nature of matter which appeals to me aesthetically though I frankly confess I have no philosophical or logical or scientific reasons to advance in support of it. I have heard it suggested that the "stuff" of which all matter is made may be electricity. Electricity may prove to be a perfectly homogeneous, non-atomic, non-elastic fluid, and the various parts of the atoms, the electrons, protons, neutrons and all the rest, may have the relationship to electricity which the whirlpools created by a canoe paddle have to the water of the lake. Each particular part of the atom might be a particular kind of infinitesimal vortex of electricity. Such a theory would account for the (probable) conversion of matter into energy and energy into matter. It would make certain facts in the physical world somewhat easier to understand. All I can say in support of it, however, is that it impresses me as being a neat and orderly way of looking at the material world.

Let the physicists ascertain the facts, and I shall be happy, without philosophical or theological prejudice, to receive the evidence. Whatever more may be discovered about the nature of matter, it will not in the slightest degree take away the reality of what we already know about extended things in common usage in the macroscopic world.

D. *The Nature of Mind*

Dualistic realism insists that there are in the world thinking things (Descartes' *res cogitans*)[15] which are not material things (Descartes' *res extensa*). Although the finite minds of our acquaintance are *local* in their primary operations, confined to the functions of their respective bodies, assisted by such mechanical devices — glasses, knives and forks and spoons, telephones, radios and other things — as may be available, the evidence seems to indicate that these thinking things, though local, are not spacially extended.

Bishop Joseph Butler in his famous *Analogy*, first published 1738,[16] pointed out that one sees with his eyes in the same sense as he sees with his glasses. One walks with his cane as well as with his feet. The body is not the mind, but an instrument used by the mind.

Cicero said long ago, "It may easily be perceived that the *mind* both sees and hears, and not those parts which are, so to speak, windows of the mind. Neither are we bodies; nor do I, while speaking this to thee, speak to thy body. What is done by the mind is done by thee."[17] Cicero also argued, "The mind of each man is the man; not that figure which may be pointed out with the finger."[18]

[15]See "Precursors of Descartes' Cogito Argument" by D. S. Robinson in his *Crucial Issues in Philosophy*, pp. 255-266. The roots of the argument are traced not only in Augustine but in Aristotle, Albertus Magnus, Thomas Aquinas and others.
[16]Part I, Chapter I, Section II.
[17]Cicero, *Tusc. Disput.* I, 20, 46 and 22, 52, quoted by Howard Malcolm, editor, in the Lippincott edition of Butler's *Analogy* published in 1886.
[18]Cicero, *de Rep.* b 6, s 24. Quoted by Malcolm, *idem*.

In Plato's *Alcibiades*, Part I, section 129, we have the following conversation:

Socrates. I will explain: The shoemaker, for example, uses a square tool, and a circular tool. And other tools for cutting?

Alcibiades. Yes.

S. But the tool is not the same as the cutter and user of the tool?

A. Of course not.

S. And in the same way the instrument of the harper is to be distinguished from the harper himself?

A. It is.

S. Now the question which I asked was whether you conceive the user to be always different from that which he uses?

A. I do.

S. Then what shall we say of the shoemaker? Does he cut with his tools or only with his hands?

A. With his hands as well.

S. He uses his hands too?

A. Yes.

S. And does he use his eyes in cutting leather?

A. He does.

S. And we admit that the user is not the same with the things which he uses?

A. Yes.

S. Then the shoemaker and the harper are to be distinguished from the hands and feet which they use?

A. Clearly.

S. Then does not a man use the whole body?

A. Certainly.

S. And that which uses is different from that which is used?

A. True.

S. Then a man is not the same as his own body?

A. That is the inference.

S. What is he, then?

A. I cannot say.

S. Nay, you can say that he is the user of the body.

A. Yes.

S. And the user of the body is the soul?

A. Yes, the soul.

S. And the soul rules?

A. Yes.

S. Let me make an assertion which will, I think, be universally admitted.

A. What is it?

S. That man is one of three things.

A. What are they?

S. Soul, body, or both together forming a whole.

A. Certainly.

S. But did we not say that the actual ruling principle of the body is man?

A. Yes, we did.

S. And does the body rule over itself?

A. Certainly not.

S. It is subject, as we were saying?

A. Yes.

S. Then that is not the principle that we are seeking?

A. It would seem not.

S. But may we say that the union of the two rules over the body, and consequently that this is the man?

A. Very likely.

S. The most unlikely of all things; for if one of the members is subject, the two united cannot possibly rule.

A. True.

S. But since neither the body, nor the union of the two, is man, either man has no real existence, or the soul is man?

A. Just so.

S. Is anything more required to prove that the soul is man?

A. Certainly not; the proof is, I think, quite sufficient. . . .

S. Then we may truly concede that you and I are conversing with one another, soul to soul?

A. Very true.

S. And that is just what I was saying before — that I, Socrates, am not arguing or talking with the face of Alcibiades, but with the real Alcibiades; or in other words, with his soul.

A. True.

S. Then he who bids a man know himself, would have him know his soul?

A. That appears to be true.

S. He whose knowledge only extends to the body, knows the things of a man, and not the man himself?

A. That is true.[19]

(1) The Mind Distinct from the Brain

Now whereas the distinction between soul and body in the platonic philosophy is coupled with the thought of degrees of reality, so that the "real" Alcibiades is the soul and not the body, it is the position of dualistic realists that, without accepting the doctrine of degrees of reality, the *distinction* between

[19]Jowett translation, Random House edition, Vol. II, pp. 764 ff.

the soul and the body, as brought out in the *Alcibiades,* may be retained.

In modern psychology and neurology the distinction between mind and body may be refined beyond the point attained by Socrates. The mind is not the brain. The "brain track" psychology has failed. If the brain were identical with the mind, a monkey trained to perform a certain trick with his right hand would be unprepared to perform the trick with his left. But this does not prove to be the case. It is a known fact that if certain parts of the brain are destroyed, and the functions corresponding to those parts impaired, the functions may be taken up by other parts of the brain. There is no exact correspondence between mind and brain. The destruction of brain tissue seems similar to what would happen if certain parts of my filing system were destroyed. It is true that my functions would be curtailed, but in part at least, I could restore the lost functions even though parts of the filing system should never be recovered. Similarly it is known that the mind can regain its functions to a considerable extent in cases in which brain tissue is completely destroyed.

(2) Biblical Terms

Up to this point we have used the terms "mind" and "soul" interchangeably. The words are not exact synonyms. They are, rather, functional designations for the non-material being which Descartes called *res cogitans.* The Bible has a wealth of psychological terms, richer than is found in ordinary English usage. There are two words for mind, *nous* and *phronema.* The former means mind in the ordinary intellectual sense. The latter designates deep reflective thought. Both are names for the non-material being of man in his intellectual relationships. The word heart, *kardia* in Greek, is not primarily an emotional term, but rather a term designating the non-material man as a whole in his moral and spiritual relationships. The will, *thelesis,* designates the non-material being of man in what we call conative aspects. Spirit, *pneuma,*[20] designates the non-material being in relationship to God without particular emphasis upon any earthly relationships. Soul, *psuche,*[21] desig-

[20]Hebrew, *ruach.*
[21]Hebrew, *nephesh.*

nates the non-material man more generally when his bodily relationships are in the context.

There are indeed trichotomists who seek to make out that the word "soul" designates a distinguishable non-material substantive entity other than "spirit," which in turn, designates another substantive entity. The facts of Biblical usage do not substantiate trichotomy. The arguments of trichotomists would lead rather to a "multotomy." There are just as good reasons for regarding the word "heart" and the *two* words for "mind," and the word "will" as designating distinguishable substantive entities. The psychological terms presented above are not synonyms, any more than son, husband and father are synonyms. Heart, mind, soul, spirit and other such words are functional nouns designating one and the same substantive entity in various functional relationships.

(3) Is the Mind Directly Known?

There are many who have argued that we are immediately conscious of the existence of our non-material being, mind or soul, without any reasoning processes leading to the inference of its existence. It is held that we know our souls just as intuitively as we know the yellow color of a dandelion when we see it. It is obviously impossible to enter into the consciousness of the individual who believes that he has intuitive knowledge of his own soul. I would suggest a word of caution, however. I believe we are on sounder ground in the opinion that the soul is known by its effects.

At the other extreme, the opposite from intuition, David Hume[22] (1711-1776) argued, at one point in his career, that we have no reason to believe in the existence of a non-material mind or soul. In Hume's *Treatise on Human Nature*, first published 1739-40, is found the oft-quoted argument against the soul.

> For my part, when I enter intimately into what I call myself, I always stumble on some particular perception or other, of heat or cold, light or shade, love or hatred, pain or pleasure. I never can catch myself at any time without a perception, and never can observe anything but the perception. When my perceptions are

[22]See my extended discussion of this point in *Philosophies of F. R. Tennant and John Dewey*, Chapter I and Appendix.

A Christian View of Being and Knowing

removed for a time, as by sound sleep, so long am I insensible of myself, and may truly be said not to exist. And were all my perceptions removed by death, and could I neither think, nor feel, nor see, nor love, nor hate, after the dissolution of my body, I should be entirely annihilated, nor do I conceive what is farther requisite to make me a perfect non-entity. If anyone upon a serious and unprejudiced reflection, thinks he has a different notion of himself, I must confess I can reason no longer with him. All I can allow him is, that he may be in the right as well as I, and that we are essentially different in this particular. He may, perhaps, perceive something simple and continued, which he calls himself; though I am certain there is no such principle in me.

These words of Hume are frequently quoted or referred to in philosophical or psychological discussions as though they were Hume's settled opinion. The fact is, however, that in an appendix to his *Treatise* Hume retracted his argument against the identity of the soul or the self. Significant words from Hume's appendix are as follows:

. . . upon a more strict review of the section concerning *personal identity*, I find myself involved in such a labyrinth, that, I must confess, I neither know how to correct my former opinions, nor how to render them consistent. . . . When I turn my reflections on *myself*, I never can perceive this *self* without some one or more perceptions; nor can I ever perceive anything but the perceptions. 'Tis the composition of these, therefore, which forms the self. . . . Philosophers begin to be reconciled to the principle, *that we have no idea of external substance, distinct from the ideas of particular qualities.* This must pave the way for a like principle with regard to the mind. *That we have no notion of it, distinct from the particular perceptions.* So far I seem to be attended with sufficient evidence. But . . . when I proceed to explain the principle of connection, which binds them [the perceptions] together, and makes us attribute to them a real simplicity and identity; I am sensible that my account is very defective. . . . If perceptions are distinct existences, they form a whole only by being connected together. But no connections among distinct existences are ever discoverable by human understanding. . . . Most philosophers seem inclined to think, that personal identity *arises* from consciousness; and consciousness is nothing but a reflected thought or perception. The present philosophy, therefore, has so far a promising aspect. But all my hopes vanish, when I come to explain the principles, that unite our successive perceptions in our thoughts or consciousness. I cannot discover any theory which gives me satisfaction on

144

this head. In short there are two principles, which I cannot render consistent . . . *that our distinct perceptions are distinct existences,* and *that the mind never perceives any real connection among distinct existences.* Did our perceptions either inhere in something simple and individual, or did the mind perceive some real connection among them, there would be no difficulty in the case. For my part, I must plead the privilege of a skeptic, and confess, that this difficulty is too hard for my understanding.

It is quite apparent that in Hume's reference to the principle of connection which binds the perceptions together, the principle that unites our successive perceptions in consciousness, he is pointing directly to the existence of a substantive mind or soul. We need not at this point delve into the mystery of memory of the past or imagination of the future. The fact is quite well known, and frequently observed in treatises on psychology, that memories, present experiences, and imaginings of the future, are, in consciousness, *my* thoughts. It is as though memory were labeled "my past experiences," and so on.

I for one would not argue that we have direct intuitive knowledge of our own minds as substantive entities. I do claim that Hume, in doubting his doubts, in asking what it is that binds together the experiences of consciousness as *my* experiences, was on the right track. These are to be taken as effects of the substantive mind or soul.

(4) Knowledge by Effects[23]

We know our minds by their effects, not only in that our states of consciousness are somehow bound together, as Hume indicated, but also in the many more or less intelligent works which we perform. It seems hardly necessary even to point to the data. When I work in my garden I am conscious of my tools and of my hands. It is completely impossible for me to resolve the visual image of my hands, my hoe and my spade into merely mental phenomena. Similarly I am conscious of

---

[23]It has been argued that the soul should be thought of as an abstract rational concept, not a substantive entity. In mathematics an equation may represent a line. $x^2 + y^2 = r^2$ is the equation for a circle whose radius is r. So, it is held, the mind or soul is only the abstract formula for the unity of personal experience. This is clever! But it confuses *implication* with *causality*. See p. 55.

putting forth mental effort, and all the data of my consciousness correlate to indicate that results are obtained by the purposive activity of which I am intuitively conscious. I can as little doubt the existence of my mind as I can doubt the existence of my hands or my tools. I plan my day's work, my semester's courses, or I take an intelligence test, as the case may be. In all such matters it is the belief of the dualistic realist that we have knowledge of such intelligence as we possess through inference from its effects.

As for our knowledge of other minds, we would agree with Berkeley that we know these other minds by their effects. It seems unnecessary to elaborate the thought. It is an obvious matter. We only regret that Berkeley did not see the consistency of the position of dualistic realism, and hold that we know material objects also by their effects.

The term realistic dualism may apply to some philosophers who do not accept the Christian view of God and the world. The grounds of our faith in God will be discussed from another point of view under the heading of epistemology. For the present purpose it must be pointed out that we believe in God because of His effects. God is not "afar off" from human experience but He has spoken in history. In the experience of Moses He named Himself "I AM." In the person of Christ, the Jesus of history, God is "manifested in the flesh." In the Bible, which we accept as God's infallible Word, we have the most complete and explicit effect of God's being and His activities. According to Christ and the Bible, nature itself is an effect of which God is the cause, and His being and characteristics may be directly inferred from the works of nature. One of the most explicit statements of this fact is found in Paul's Epistle to the Romans, chapter 1, verse 20: "His invisible attributes, His eternal power and divine character, from the creation of the cosmos, being known by the things which He made, are clearly seen, so that they [who turn away from Him] are without excuse."[24]

[24]My own translation.

E. *Causality*

The category of cause and effect was discussed at considerable length in Chapter II, the chapter on the categories. It was found necessary to go into some detail in order to make clear what this category is in common discourse. The student should at this point review pages 54 ff. on "The Category of Causation." In the subsequent chapters causality has been taken for granted. Belief in causality is not confined to adherents of dualistic realism. It is assumed in most systems of materialism and in most systems of idealism. However, since causality is sometimes denied, it is necessary that a discussion of causality shall form a part of this chapter. Causality is regarded as an actually existing relationship between substantive entities.

(1) Mechanical Causation

For the great majority of human beings, mechanical causation has not been thought of as a mystery. Matter and force are in constant interplay of causal relationships. Mechanical causation in the material world is so easy to apprehend that there have been many materialists who have gone to the extreme, and who adhere to a dogmatic mechanistic philosophy of causality governing the totality of experience. This attitude has been referred to in the chapter on materialism.

On the other hand, in our generation, physicists have begun to talk about a principle of *indeterminacy*. Werner Karl Heisenberg's book, *Physikalischen Prinzipien der Quantum Theorie,* was published in 1930. In it he indicated that the behavior of the electron in its orbit in the atom cannot be predicted. It is impossible, with our present means of measurement, to determine both the position and the velocity of the same electron at the same time. Heisenberg did not declare that the electron has free will, or that it is essentially indeterminate. He merely pointed out that its behavior cannot be predicted by present means. No one knows just when, or whether, means will be devised whereby the behavior of the electron can be precisely predicted.

The Heisenberg principle, or the principle of indeterminacy, has been taken up[25] by certain philosophers, and made out to be a principle of free will in the material universe. An enormous amount of popular writing has been circulated on this subject. On the one hand mechanistic materialists argue that the behavior of the electron is not known to be indeterminate, but is only at the present time undetermined. On the other hand many idealists, pantheists and other types have been inclined to assert dogmatically that the principle of free will is a principle now proved to prevail within the material world.

It is obvious that in the physical world we can predict with a remarkable degree of accuracy the behavior of atoms in the macroscopic aggregate. This is done on a principle similar to that which governs actuarial mathematics. Insurance companies cannot predict when one individual will come to the end of his life, but they can, with reasonable accuracy, predict the number of persons per thousand who will die within a given time in a large population. So it is that, allowing for the undetermined, or what is popularly called the principle of indeterminacy, we can count on the reasonable regularity of the mechanical world and at the same time, if it pleases our fancy, we can imagine that the various parts of the atom are not completely within a mechanical causal system, but that at least some of the parts have free will.

I can only say that, whereas, as a Christian, I of course reject the mechanistic view of the totality of the universe, yet on the other hand, although I have no evidence, I sincerely hope that the principle of indeterminacy will not prevail in scientific thought concerning the material world. I hope that

[25]The student will find an interesting defense of "relative" personal indeterminism, alleged to be analogous to the indeterminacy of the electron, in an article entitled "Freedom Requires Indeterminism and Universal Causality" by Charles Hartshorne of Emory University, in the *Journal of Philosophy* for September 11, 1958, Vol. LV, No. 19. I am not at all convinced. For one thing, Hartshorne seems to me to destroy all ethical values by denying the perduring numerical identity of a personal being. He says that as "physics has now discredited the notion of electrons as enduring individuals identical through time," so, ". . . the locus of freedom is not in the enduring ego, but in the self here and now. . . . The decider of a present issue . . . is a new decider. . . . For we are as we act and we act as we are." Where then is ethical responsibility? Nevertheless, Hartshorne's argument on indeterminism is well worth examining.

the atoms and all their parts are completely within a mechanical causal system. My philosophy of the moral responsibility of personal beings is not in the slightest degree assisted by a wishful doctrine of free will inside the atom.

(2) Psychological Causation

It would seem that within the sphere of psychological events there ought to be no question of the actuality of the causal relationship. We are immediately conscious of formulating purposes and putting them into action. It seems to be an immediate datum, like the color of the dandelion when one sees it, that we have effective ability to form purposes and effective ability, at least in our minds, to carry them out.

There have been those, like Leibnitz, who have denied the reality of causality in human psychology. Leibnitz and Berkeley denied all secondary causes and held that God is the only real cause. Denial of human psychological causality has not been a widely accepted doctrine. Even Hume believed in cause as a relationship among ideas. He regarded association of ideas as the *cause* of the "absurd" idea of causality in the material world.

The great battle over causality in psychology has not been over the question of the reality of the causal relationship, but over the question of free will. Are *all* psychological events rigidly controlled within a total causal system? Or is there an area of freedom? Is there an area in which the individual mind may act spontaneously, in such a way as to be itself ultimately responsible for certain of its actions?

There are influential philosophers, some of them Bible-believing Christians, who hold that there is no freedom in the psychological world. The denial of freedom in psychology is usually called "determinism," as the denial of freedom in the material world is usually called "mechanism." The usage of the two terms is not rigidly distinguishable.

In psychological determinism it is held that every thought, every psychological process, is totally within a rigid causal system, without the slightest degree of spontaneity possible on the part of the thinker. It is argued that if one knew all the factors of heredity and environment brought to bear upon one's psychology, one could predict his minutest thoughts and his total mental activity, just as one could, in mechanics, predict the revolutions of the wheels of a machine.

The denial of free will proceeds not only from those who deny the existence of a soul as a substantive entity, or who wish to regard all reality as a vast mechanism. The denial of free will proceeds also from a certain type of theology. In Bible doctrine we learn that God "worketh all things after the counsel of his own will" (Ephesians 1:11). This, and other Scriptures, are put together in the comprehensive definition of "The Decrees of God" in the *Westminster Shorter Catechism:* "The decrees of God are his eternal purpose according to the counsel of his will whereby for his own glory he hath foreordained whatsoever comes to pass." We learn also that the atonement of Christ was accomplished, not for the mere hypothetical salvation of a people who might happen to accept him, but, as Dr. Machen used to say, "He died *to save a people.*" His people are "chosen . . . in him before the foundation of the world" (Ephesians 1:4). From the Scriptural doctrine of election there follows the doctrine of "the perseverance of the saints." That is, the Scriptural doctrine that those who are chosen in Christ before the foundation of the world, are infallibly going to decide for Him, in faith, which is "the gift of God" (Ephesians 2:8). And those who put their faith in Him are infallibly going on to share in His eternal glory.

It is my contention that, contrary to the opinions of some estimable Christians, these Scriptural doctrines are not in the slightest degree contrary to the psychological fact of free will and human responsibility.

As a believer in free will and spontaneity in human psychology, I must first of all give a warning, to the effect that free will can be grossly exaggerated. If we take time to analyze the social and physiological factors which are brought to bear upon what we consider our ordinary decisions, the area in which we can believe ourselves to be free is stringently reduced. Our speech, our clothing, our food, our total culture are given us from the outside, and are generally accepted by the individual without much modification.

Furthermore, it must be pointed out that free will does not mean the power of capricious choice. Professor Fullerton in his *Introduction to Philosophy*, referred to above, says that he does not wish to have anyone with free will for a neighbor, because he could not tell what the neighbor might do next. He defines free will as the power of capricious choice. He thinks the neighbor might live next to him for fifty years in all kindliness and courtesy, and the very next morning the same neighbor might turn into a cheat and even a murderer. Nothing could be farther from the conception of free will here advocated. There are, of course, many temporary and superficial decisions in the process of a real decision. Also, changes of circumstances require new decisions. But underneath the superficial choices, our permanent choices are exercised through a *process of time*, and gradually *become binding* upon us. There is a point in our experience at which a genuine decision is reached. Every such point of decision is preceded by a process of coming to a decision. Once a decision is genuinely arrived at, it becomes a part of our habits, and a part of our character. Insofar as a decision is genuine, it is not to be reversed.

The fact that a genuine choice, a genuine decision, involves an actual irreversible change in one's character, perfectly harmonizes with, and supplements the doctrine of the "perseverance of the saints." Moreover, the psychological analysis of the process of decision does not rule out, or deny, the work of the Holy Spirit in convicting, converting, regenerating, and "working faith in us." These are two aspects of one process.

The experience of Saul of Tarsus in reaching a decision on the road to Damascus illustrates what takes place when a decision is genuinely reached. At one moment he was riding forward with a firm purpose to destroy the Christian church. Then there was the flash and the voice from the heavenly glory. Paul replied, "Who art thou, Lord?" The second time came the voice from heaven, identifying Jesus as the speaker.

At Saul's second reply, "Lord, what wilt thou have me to do?" his decision had been reached.

We should do slight justice to the record if we supposed that the instant on the road to Damascus constituted the entire process of decision. The very words, "It is hard for thee to kick against the goads," prove that he had been in a state of spiritual conflict, as one item of evidence after another was borne in upon his mind. Certainly there was a process leading up to the decision. Just as certainly there was a process of organization and consolidation following the decision. Saul's character was changed. He became Paul, the great apostle. Thus we see that the exercise of free will is not to be identified as capricious choice.

The worst of it is that a wrong decision, when finally made, is not reversed. It is recorded in Mark 3:29 that Jesus said those who called the work of God the work of an unclean spirit were "guilty of eternal sin."[26] The psychological implication of Jesus' saying in this context is that when men have observed the work of God's Holy Spirit through Jesus Christ in the lives of men, and have deliberately called this the work of "an unclean spirit" they have made a permanent choice against the grace of God. They will never change.

The psychological fact of the process, and the permanency of a genuine decision is observable in human conduct. As we deal with those who have not yet accepted Christ, we should realize that they are men who, so far as our knowledge goes, are in the process of making a decision for time and eternity. Each time they postpone the acceptance of Christ, it becomes more and more difficult for them to decide for Him. This is the meaning of the solemn warning in the first verses of the second chapter of Hebrews, "lest we drift away."[27] Those whom we are seeking to win will at some point, perhaps known to God alone, make a final decision which will be a part of their eternal character. The teaching now being emphasized, that a decision involves a process and

[26]The ordinary English translation, "in danger of eternal damnation," is based upon inferior manuscript evidence.
[27]The English translation, "lest we let them slip," is not as vivid as the Greek words.

is ultimately irreversible, is not in any way contrary to the fact that a decision is made at a point in time. But whereas we recognize, and we seek to press home, the importance of the point of decision, it is of the greatest importance for those who are engaged in gospel work to recognize that every hour, every moment in all social, business and personal relationships, those with whom we deal are in the process of making the supreme decision for or against the grace of God in Christ. Or if they have made the final decision, they are in the process of developing its eternal implications.

It is important to note that according to the Bible, the decision for Christ is not a creditable good work. "It is not of him that willeth . . . but of God that sheweth mercy" (Romans 9:16). It is the Holy Spirit of God who energizes within us both the willing and the doing of God's good pleasure (Philippians 2:13). The creditable cause of the salvation of one who is saved, is solely the grace of God. Faith is the *if*, not the *because*. Many times in the New Testament we are told that we are saved *"through* faith." Never is one said to be saved *on the grounds of faith.*[28]

The question is asked, If faith is "the gift of God" (Ephesians 2:8), how can it be said to be also a responsible personal decision? The serious inquirer should study the great chapter on faith in Vol. III of Hodge's *Systematic Theology.* Faith is indeed an act of man, but it is an act impossible except by the grace of God. It is the function of the Holy Spirit of God to convict the lost individual *and to enable him to believe.*

A simple illustration may be helpful. A child playing under an apple tree cannot[29] reach the apples and may not be the least interested. An adult picks the child up, calls his attention to the apples and holds him in a position where, if he will, he can partake. So the Holy Spirit *convicts* the

[28]"Through faith" is expressed by a genitive with the Greek preposition *dia*, or the preposition *ek*, also with a genitive. "On the grounds of faith" would be expressed by the accusative case with the preposition *dia*. Frequently salvation is said to be *dia pisteos*, genitive; never *dia pistin*, accusative.

[29]Calvin's point (*Institutes*, Bk. II, Ch. II) in saying that the lost are "despoiled of freedom of will" is just this, that man cannot please God (Romans 8:8) without the enablement of grace. He does not deny free will in the sense of responsibility for rejecting the offer of grace. See Bk. III, Ch. XXIV.

world. In such a simple case there is no credit to the individual who takes the fruit, but there is a definite responsibility upon him who will not take.

This leads to the fact that, in the Scriptures throughout, the pattern of praise or blame for human decision is definitely *not symmetrical*. The creditable cause of the salvation of the saved is solely the grace of God. In all eternity we shall be more and more *amazed* at the Saviour's "amazing grace" which saved us. On the other hand, the chargeable cause of the loss of the lost is entirely within himself.[30] It is *"because of the fact that [Gr. 'oti]* he has not believed" that he is condemned; and this "because" is analyzed by the further statement that "light has come into the world, and men loved darkness rather than light, because their deeds were evil" (John 3:18, 19).

One may, of course, reject the doctrine of free will and moral responsibility, but if one rejects, he does so willfully and without reason. All the evidence is on the other side. Furthermore, there can be no possible doubt within the Christian horizon, because according to the Biblical view of things, God Himself, in His infinite wisdom, is definitely angry (John 3:36) with those who ultimately refuse His grace in Christ.

I would urge then that the psychological world is characterized by a combination of free will, or spontaneity, and causality, so that the individual, among the various causal factors and motivations with which he has to do, is responsible for his ultimate moral choices.

(3) Causality in God's Character and in His Will

In discussing the matter of causality in the realm of mind or spirit, it is appropriate to ask for an intelligible view of causality in the nature and in the will of God. Historically, there have been extremes on both sides. Some of our contemporaries argue that the laws of logic, mathematics and ethics, are sheer creations of the arbitrary will of God. It is held that if God should decree that two plus two should be five, that would then be the case. Similarly, if God should decree that it is right and proper for a man to bear false

---

[30]Calvin (*Institutes*, Bk. III, Ch. XXIV) argues that "the destination of the reprobate is procured by themselves."

witness against his neighbor, false witness would then be ethically good. Charles Hodge[31] quotes Descartes as saying that the reason why the three angles of a plane triangle equal two right angles is that God willed it to be so. According to this view, there would be within the character of God no principle of consistency, but all would be purely arbitrary and capricious free will.

At the other extreme no less a theologian than Jonathan Edwards (1703-1758) in his famous essay on *The Will* argues that God has no freedom of will whatsoever, but is completely bound by the laws of logic and ethics. Edwards was a marvelous pastor and evangelist and personal worker, but philosophically he was a rationalistic idealist, adhering rigidly to the "law of sufficient reason" not only for the creature, but also for the Creator Himself.

According to the Biblical view, God is not subject to any factors, forces or laws external to Himself, but the Biblical writers constantly refer to the *character* of God as immutable. God's character of truth makes it "impossible for God to lie" (Hebrews 6:18; Titus 1:2; II Timothy 2:13). As Christians, the basis of our standards of ethics is the revealed will of God, but we are informed in the Scriptures that the will of God expresses the immutable and consistent character of God.

I suggest that we regard the laws of mathematics and logic as derived, either by discovery or by direct revelation, from the very character of God Himself. Since God's character is the truth, anyone who tries to act upon the assumption that the three angles of a plane triangle are not equal to two right angles, will be fighting not only against the abstract laws of logic, but also against the character of God.

On the other hand, there are brute facts of which we must take account. The term "brute fact" does not mean irrational or anti-logical fact. Such would of course be impossible; but the term brute fact means fact which is not caused by, or necessarily derived from, logical principles. The first great brute fact, and the most important brute fact of

[31]*Systematic Theology*, Vol. I, p. 409. Hodge, of course, disagrees with Descartes on this point.

all, is the fact of God's existence. The being of God is *not caused by anything*. He simply and eternally *is*.

A second brute fact of tremendous importance is the existence of the created world. According to the Bible there is no reason why God had to create a universe of finite beings. In the unity and complexity of the triune God there was no necessity for a finite creation. Of His own free will He chose to create the finite universe.

A third brute fact, and this the most amazing of all, is that He chose to redeem a people out of the fallen mass of self-corrupted humanity. There is no logical necessity for the redemptive program of God in Christ. "Of his own will begat he us with the word of truth, that we should be a kind of first-fruits of his creatures" (James 1:18). It would have been perfectly just and perfectly logical if the terrible curse of the imprecatory Psalms (see especially Psalm 69) had been poured out upon the sinful race. But He chose "of his mere good pleasure" to save a people. This is why we sing, "Amazing Grace," and we expect the amazement to increase as the ages roll by and as more and more of His grace is understood.

We hold then that causality and spontaneity are both operative principles in the realm of minds and spirits, and that both causality and spontaneity in the realm of spirits are characteristics of the ontological sphere of ethics.

(4) Causal Interaction

Interaction between mind and body has been discussed to some extent in the chapter on materialism. It is in the area of interaction between matter and mind that the greatest difficulties about causality have arisen. In his article on causality[32] F. R. Tennant refers to the "scholastic" notion that causal interaction is possible only within the homogeneous. Tennant gives no references, and I have been unable to trace the source of this view. It is held that causality is conceivable if all is mind, or, on the other hand, causality is conceivable if all is matter, but it is held to be inconceivable that there should be causal interaction between heterogeneous

[32]In Hastings' *Encyclopaedia of Religion and Ethics*, referred to above.

substantive entities such as mind and matter. I have found this view taken for granted in the writings of numerous prominent philosophers, but I have never found the slightest reason given in support of this assumption.

To me it would seem that the very notion of causality implies otherness, at least numerical otherness. Knowing a little of the ordinary laws of mechanics, we can understand physical causal relationships between croquet balls and mallets. We can also assimilate the notion of causality between minds and thoughts. In all cases, however, the cause and effect are conceived as numerically other. It would seem to me that qualitative otherness as well as numerical otherness would be perfectly harmonious with the concept of causality. I must, for lack of any reason to the contrary, put down the notion that causality is possible only betwen homogeneous entities, as a pure irrational prejudice.

It is true that disciples of Descartes, because of what I believe to be an erroneous interpretation of Descartes' dualism, brought forward a doctrine called occasionalism. It was held that there can be no genuine interaction in the created world, but that when one event seems to cause another, God is the actual immediate cause. The doctrine of pre-established harmony brought forth by Leibnitz differs from the doctrine of occasionalism in that causality was accounted for not by continuous miracles, but by one miracle of pre-established relationships.

Contrary to such view, Descartes himself taught that there is causal interaction between mind and body. Descartes thought that this interaction was centered in the pineal gland which is located at the base of the brain.

Those who are attached to a mechanistic view of the material world are inclined to reject causality in interaction between mind and body on the ground of their theory of a "closed system." There is a strong tendency to regard the material world as a closed system, such that nothing new is put into it and nothing goes out of it. To admit, therefore, that a thought in the mind can be the cause of a physical movement seems quite impossible. I have referred elsewhere[33] to the arguments of Hodge, Locke and Tennant, showing that we are immediately conscious of putting forth effort and obtaining results. And I have discussed[34] Hume's lame argument against this obvious fact.

But, says the mechanistic philosopher, it is *inconceivable* that thought, or mental purpose, should add to, or subtract from, the sum total of the forces operating in the material world. Therefore, it is held, there can be no interaction.

The late William McDougall of Duke University, in his type of psychology, which he designated by the Greek adjective *hormic*,[35] frequently discussed the nature of mental and physical interaction. He used a number of illustrations such as the fact that the manipulation of the accelerator of an automobile does not add to, or subtract from, the power by which the machine is propelled, but only releases that power. I believe the term *trigger action* conveys a correct idea of the nature of interaction between mind and body. In the pressing of a trigger not the slightest addition is made to the stored up energy in the cartridge. The trigger may be pressed by the finger of a giant, or the finger of a child. Releasing the spring of the trigger does not break into the system of mechanical operation of the cartridge with its projectile.

It is not necessary to deny that the material universe may be regarded as a closed system. In fact, I am inclined to think (wishfully, I admit) that it is a closed system. All that is necessary is to recognize that through the human nervous system the physico-chemical energy stored up in the human anatomy may be *released* in appropriate times and manners, in accordance with the ethical purposive consciousness of a human spirit.

Santayana and other epiphenomenalists deny that thought can produce changes in the material world, but it is not difficult for them to see that material causes do produce changes in consciousness. To me the mystery seems just as great, while

[33]Pp. 54 f., above.
[34]*Philosophies of F. R. Tennant and John Dewey*, pp. 28 ff.
[35]From the Greek word *horme*, meaning "the putting forth of effort."

of course the fact is just as obvious, in the one case as in the other. We can trace the physical impulse from the sensory nerve endings to the specialized portions of the brain which we know are connected with sensation. But when we have traced the impact of a ray of light through the cornea and the lens to the retina, and from the retina of the eye to the optic lobe, we still have failed to come to the slightest degree of consciousness. It is simply a fact, mysterious though it may be, that consciousness occurs — that the human nervous system is so constructed that physical events, without necessarily breaking the closed physical system, produce mental events. This the epiphenomenalists admit. It is also a fact, one of the commonest of elementary immediate intuitive experiences, that conscious purpose releases mechanical energy stored up in the muscles and produces changes in the material world.

(5) Mental Causality Without Bodily Means?

We have discussed (1) causality in the material realm, (2) causality in the psychological realm, (3) causality in the character and in the will of God, and (4) causality in interaction between mind and body. At this point the question arises, can the human mind interact with the material world except through its body? This involves three sub-questions: Is there extra-sensory human perception of the material world? Is there action of human mind upon matter except through its body? Is mental telepathy actually experienced between human minds?

It is not my purpose to discuss the so-called evidence advanced in support of the affirmative answers to this triple question. I have read a considerable amount of it, and I am not in the least impressed. My answer is wholly in the negative. The positive evidence for two-way interaction between the human mind and body seems as clear as daylight. So-called evidence for the psychological occult is as obscure as midnight.

Philosophically, however, I must point out that this is a question of fact, and not a question of principle. There is no *a priori* reason against incorporeal interaction of minds with material things, and with other minds. We believe in God as an incorporeal Spirit, governing the world of men and things in His works of providence. We believe in personal immortality apart from the body, in heavenly fellowship, pending the resurrection. We believe in silent, as well as audible prayer.

It seems to me a matter of *fact* that the human mind interacts with the material world and with other finite persons through its body, and through its body only, as long as it is in the body. On this assumption the data of experience integrate more and more fruitfully, as experience increases in breadth and depth. On the assumption of the psychological occult, as I have observed human behavior, experience grows more and more confused, frustrating and disintegrative.

Conclusion

Dualistic realism is not a philosophy which, as John Dewey always accuses, fixes a "great gulf" between mind and matter. Dualistic realism is committed to integrated interactionism in the material realm, in the psychological realm, and between the two realms.

Dualistic realism is not committed to the view that the total universe is rigidly bound within a deterministic or mechanistic causal system. It is my personal opinion that the material universe is so bound, but in this I might be mistaken. Unless one believes that something comes from nothing, the eternal existent in the past, whether God, or atheous process, must be uncaused. It is my position that, while causality operates in the realm of spirit and mind, yet spontaneity operates also, with causality, in this realm. The combination of causality and spontaneity in the spiritual realm is essential to our concept of ethical responsibility.

We present then an integrated view of metaphysics. The really existing world is an interacting system. Extended things are real. Thinking beings are real. Interaction is real. God has created all, and we as men are ultimately responsible to Him.

160

PART III

EPISTEMOLOGY, THE THEORY OF KNOWING

CHAPTER VI

BETWEEN ONTOLOGY AND EPISTEMOLOGY

Ontology and epistemology cannot be separated. Principal James Iverach of Aberdeen says, "Historically we find that philosophy begins with Metaphysics. . . . From the historical point of view, Epistemology is a critical reflection on Metaphysics."[1] It seems best at this point to mention briefly a number of topics which lie between metaphysics and epistemology. It happens that in each case it has been decided not to devote a separate chapter, in an introductory book of this kind, to the extended discussion of the topic.

A. *Secondary Qualities*

In discussing the categories it was pointed out that what Locke called "secondary qualities," that is qualities like color, resonance, taste, and that sort of thing, are best regarded as relationships between material situations and non-material minds. It will not be necessary here to repeat much of what was said. But it is important to call attention to these matters as we begin the discussion of the theory of knowledge.

It has been pointed out that when we say redness is in the rose itself, we refer to a physical situation in which ordinary sunlight is reflected from the rose in a certain wave length. When we say redness is in the mind, we mean that the mind, receiving the optical impression of the given wave length, has an experience which we call the observation of redness. Both the objective and the subjective definitions are intelligible, if they are kept distinct. For clarity it is thought best unless otherwise specified, to define redness not as the physical situation in the rose, and not as the mental experience, but as the relationship between the two. A similar position was taken with reference to other secondary qualities.

[1]Hastings' E. R. E. Article, "Epistemology," Vol. V., pp. 337-356.

Professor Durant Drake quotes Professor Cohen to the effect that *"all* qualities are essentially relational."[2] I should not go so far; but Drake's argument against the view that *some* qualities are relational, to me is not convincing. A discussion of secondary qualities, then, lies in a field between ontology and epistemology.

B. *Values, Aesthetics*

Some writers apply the term "tertiary qualities" to qualities upon which we place values. I suggest that the entire subject of value lies in both the field of ontology and the field of epistemology. Aesthetics involves the value which we call beauty. I would class aesthetics with other value fields, as one of the in-between subjects.

Philosophers have written learned essays and extended books on the philosophy of beauty. As for myself, I should prefer to have the student take good courses in "music appreciation" and "art appreciation" from those who are specially competent in their respective fields.

Dualistic realism is not committed to a detailed theory of aesthetics, but it is held that beauty is objectively real in the created world in the same sense in which secondary qualities are objectively real. Similarly, beauty is also subjectively real. But for clarity, beauty should be defined as a relationship between the objective situation and minds capable of appreciating it.

C. *Ethics*

The distinctive features of Christian ethics were mentioned in the Introduction, and the place of ethics in the family of sciences was presented in Chapter I. It has not been possible, within the compass of this book, to include an extended chapter on the subject. My books, *Sin and Atonement* and *The Christian Life*[3] took up basic questions of Christian ethics from the Biblical point of view.

Whereas the Christian message has much to say about details of ethical conduct, yet the Christian message has far

[2]*Essays in Critical Realism*, pp. 17 ff.
[3]Zondervan, 1936-37, volumes III and IV in *The Lamb of God* series.

more to say about the basic principles of the holiness of God, the moral corruption of the human race, and the plan of salvation from sin through Christ, than about the details of practice.

Principles of Christian ethics are based upon the will of God as revealed in the Bible. The will of God expresses the holy character of God as the ultimate source of moral distinction. Involving conviction and faith as a response, ethics, too, lies between ontology and epistemology.

D. *Social Values, Economics*

Sociology and economics are fields in which some philosophers place major emphasis. These are favorite subjects of mine, but I would not bring them into a general textbook in philosophy except to point out certain fundamental principles.

The values of human society are definitely in the area which lies between ontology and epistemology. This would seem obvious from the merely human point of view. From the Biblical, creationist, viewpoint it is of the greatest importance. Christianity teaches that the purposes of God are concerned not merely with the individual, but with the social group. God has historically dealt with a visible people, called the church, in different ages, a society "within," but not "of," the society of the world;[4] separate and distinct, yet integrated with the common responsibilities of mankind. It is an outstanding distinctive of Christianity that the church is commissioned to spread the good news of the Christian message to all the peoples of the world, and to bring as many as possible within the society of the redeemed.

Economics is a major part of the group of disciplines called the social sciences. From the point of view of Christian philosophy it is important to call the student's attention to the fact that values in the field of economics are both material and spiritual. Christ commanded His disciples, with reference to the hungry multitudes, "Give ye them to eat" (Mark 6:37), and He made it possible to feed them. He also said, "Man shall not live by bread alone" (Luke 4:4); and, "A man's

[4]John 17:15, 16.

165

life consisteth not in the abundance of the things which he possesseth" (Luke 12:15). Economic values are exchange values, basically, the values of the market. But economic values are not solely of the body. When God said to fallen man, "In the sweat of thy face shalt thou eat bread" (Genesis 3:19), I believe it was largely for the discipline of the spirit and for the developing of the understanding, that economic burdens were placed upon us.

The greatest text in Christendom in the field of economics is found in Paul's Epistle to the Ephesians, "Let him that stole steal no more: but rather let him labour, working with his hands the thing which is good, that he may have to give to him that needeth" (Ephesians 4:28).

E. *Learning*

Learning as such is not usually listed with the valuational studies, but I believe it belongs in this category. The student should diligently study the Book of Proverbs to ascertain the correct place of learning as between ontology and epistemology.

Learning is not merely a matter of educational psychology. The content of learning is objective. It lies in the world of material and spiritual substantive entities and relationships. But the acquiring of learning requires an attitude which I think definitely belongs within the field of epistemology. "Wherefore is there a price in the hand of the fool to get wisdom, seeing he hath no heart to it?" (Proverbs 17:16) Professor John Bailey, writing an autobiographical essay in *Contemporary American Theology*,[5] spoke of his early school training in the Scottish Highlands. "My masters," he said, "had minds richly stored with various knowledge . . ." By way of comparison, he remarks, "I was fortunate in my masters. Since those days I have made acquaintance with a kind of schoolmaster who is greatly skilled in the mechanics of his profession and knows all there is to know . . . about how to teach — but who has little or nothing to impart! Of this

[5]Vergilius Ferm, ed. second series, Round Table Press, 1933.

kind of dominie[6] it can truly be said that, if only he knew anything, his pupils in time would come to know it also."

I am not speaking against pedagogical methods, and neither was Professor John Bailey; but I would take this occasion to put in a plea for a greater appreciation of learning among us all, and for at least a few outstanding men in every community with well-stocked, well-balanced, learned minds.

[6]Dominie is the Scottish term for the schoolmaster. Among the Dutch the dominie is the minister.

CHAPTER VII

A PRIORI THEORIES OF EPISTEMOLOGY

As the term *a priori* signifies reasoning from that which is prior, *a priori* theories of epistemology are inclined to assert that there must be definite prior principles, or facts, or systems, accepted as the basis of knowledge, if valid knowledge is to be had.

The opposite of the term *a priori* is of course *a posteriori*. Since *a priori* reasoning is deductive, that is, it reasons down from generalities, the opposite of *a priori* reasoning is frequently called "inductive." Inductive[1] reasoning builds up from particulars toward general conclusions.

A priori reasoning has a certain advantage in that no inductivist would think of disputing the fact that if there is to be valid reasoning, there must be the acceptance of the general principles of logic. The difference lies not in the recognition of the necessity of general principles, but in the necessity of placing these principles in a specified order of procedure. The apriorist holds that the general principles must come first and there is no leading up to them. The inductivist, on the other hand, in dealing with individuals who wish to know the truth, who are seeking after knowledge — that is, who are in need of an epistemology — is willing to take the individuals where he finds them, accept such scraps of broken truth as they may possess, show the individuals the fallacy of their errors, and lead them as best he can into a knowledge of the truth.

There are several forms of apriorism with which we have to do. (1) One type of apriorist says, "You must accept the Bible as the infallible Word of God, or there is nothing more we can discuss." (2) Another type of apriorist says, "You must

[1]See the article "What is Induction" by Charles A. Fritz, Jr. of the U. of Conn. in the *Journal of Philosophy* for Feb. 18, 1960, Vol. LVII No. 4.

believe in the sovereign, triune God first of all, or there is no way whereby we can talk together intelligently." (3) The rationalistic apriorist says, "You must accept the system of reason as outlined in the logic which I give you (usually including Leibnitz' law of sufficient reason) or I cannot talk with you further." By way of contrast[2] the inductivist[3] says, "I believe in the sovereign, triune God and I shall endeavor to persuade you to believe in Him. I believe the Bible is the infallible Word of God and I shall give you my reasons in the hope that you may come to the same conclusion. I believe in the laws of logic and I will try to help you see the importance of logical principles."

The inductivist then proceeds to discover what fragments of truth the inquirer may have. He shows how any fragment of truth is inconsistent with falsehood. He seeks to help the inquirer to reject falsehood and accept *the* truth.

A. *The Biblical A Priori*

Professor Warren Young in his excellent *Christian Approach to Philosophy* takes a position which he calls "Christian realism" and which scarcely differs from what I have called dualistic realism, but Professor Young presents Christian realism as though it were something quite different from empiricism. Now, in my *Philosophies of F. R. Tennant and John Dewey* I took considerable pains to present the history of the term empiricism, and its usage in good literature. Briefly, empiricism simply means learning from experience. The word has been used by reputable writers to *include divine revelation,* by immediate, as well as by historical and natural processes. It is quite incorrect to imply that empiricism and faith in revelation are, in any way, incompatible or conflicting systems.

One epistemological trait is characteristic of the Biblical

[2]The topic here discussed is not the *tactics* of psychological persuasion, but the reasoning approach to be used with the serious minded, open minded inquirer.
[3]I have stated the traditional arguments for the existence of God at considerable length in *What Is God?* (Zondervan, 1936-37). In my pamphlet on *Thomas and the Bible* I have given my criticisms of the Thomistic form of the arguments.

writers throughout, that is the appeal to empirical evidence in verification of the divine authority of their message. In the tenth chapter of the Gospel according to John it is recorded that Jesus was accused of blasphemy because He said, "I am the Son of God," thus, in the Jewish way of thinking, "making himself equal[4] with God." His reply is in two steps. (1) Man is created in the image of God. There is a God-related element, even in fallen man (Psalm 82:6, 7). Therefore Jesus' claim to be God in the flesh *might* be true. It is *not necessarily* blasphemy. (2) Jesus next appealed to the empirical evidence "If I do not the works of my Father, believe me not. But if I do, though ye believe not me, believe the works: that ye may come to know, and continue to know,[5] that the Father is in me, and I in him" (vss. 37, 38).

Compare the empirical evidence for the resurrection of Christ cited in the fifteenth chapter of I Corinthians, and the reference to "many infallible proofs" in Acts 1:3.

A prominent Christian philosophy teacher, an apriorist, whose sincere faith I do not question, was once lecturing to a group of science teachers, vigorously attacking the scientific inductive method of reasoning. In the discussion period which followed, I challenged the lecturer to make any positive statement with regard to objective facts concerning any substantive entities. I said that I could show that his destructive arguments would apply against any factual statement he might make.

The speaker replied immediately, "The Bible is the infallible Word of God."

I then asked him when he had ever seen a Bible, how he knew it was a Bible, and what evidence he could give to show that he had had a Bible in his hands.

The point is that, apart from empirical evidence, we have no such thing as revelation, no such thing as the Bible. As a matter of fact in Bible schools and seminaries in which the Bible is unquestioningly accepted as the infallible Word

[4]John 10:30-39. Cf. John 5:18.
[5]The force of the Greek tenses, the ingressive aorist and the continuous present, is missed in the common English translation.

of God, classroom lectures always take up the *reasons why* we believe the Bible. "Evidences" is a standard course in Bible-believing schools.

Certainly if we are dealing with those who already believe the Bible, we can save much time by simply going forward to develop the doctrines and the implications which the Bible sets forth.

It is also true that, in dealing with unbelievers, there are many times when it is impractical to take time to develop the arguments for the Bible. There are many times when psychological strategy calls for a simple affirmation from the Bible, and frequently relevant truths from the Bible will carry their own weight and produce conviction. This fact is of course in itself one of the empirical evidences.

But we are not here discussing the practical strategy, or the psychology of personal work. The *causes* of belief are manifold. The causes of faith include the friendly attitude, the honest voice, and everything which goes with the legitimate process of persuasion.

But this is a chapter on epistemology, and we are asking what are the *grounds* of our belief. The empiricist, or the individual who believes in the practical use of inductive evidence, claims that we have abundant evidence for our faith in the Bible.

B. *The Theistic A Priori*

As Christians, we begin not with the evidences for the existence of God but with the assumption of God's existence. We proclaim and expound the doctrine of the Trinity. We preach Christ; and we give exegesis of the doctrine of the Holy Spirit. We seldom touch upon the evidences for the life of Jesus as God manifest in the flesh in our ordinary preaching and teaching, although the deity of Christ is a subject more frequently argued than evidences for the existence of God.

The common Christian practice in regard to theistic evidences is analogous to the ordinary practice with reference to the existence of the sun, the existence of the material world, or any other matter of commonly accepted fact. It would be absurd to take the time of young people in the elementary schools, the high schools, the colleges, or the graduate schools, with evidences for the existence of the sun, for the simple reason that they all believe that the sun is there.

However, if we had to deal with a Sunday school picnic of Christian Scientist young people who do not believe in the dangers of sunburn, we might well take time for evidences of the existence of the sun, and we should not be at all at a loss to marshal those evidences. Similarly, when we deal with idealists who do not believe in the existence of the material world, we have our evidences. When we deal with persons who do not believe in hygiene or sanitation, we have our evidences for the existence of infectious germs.

Those of us who believe in the validity of the arguments for the existence of God, are not attempting to show that the Christian apologetic must always begin with theistic evidences. We know that a great multitude of humanity are not committed to the denial of the existence of God, and are ready to believe that He exists, if His character and His plan of redemption are made plain and simple.

On the other hand, we are dealing with a considerable number of people in the world who are intellectually committed to positions antagonistic to Christian theism. There are not very many out-and-out atheists, but there are many who have been instructed in the idea that God is an impersonal principle, or a pantheistic influence. When we speak to people of this kind in terms of our Christian faith in God our Heavenly Father, Christ the eternal Son of God, the Holy Spirit as the Third Person of the Trinity, it is frequently necessary to outline our reasons for faith in the God of the Bible. Just as we have good reasons for believing in the existence of the sun, and governing ourselves accordingly, so we have, from the Bible, and from the experiences of those who have believed the Bible down through the centuries, good and useful arguments pointing to the existence of God as the Bible proclaims Him.

It is one thing to say, "Arguing from theistic evidences

is often not the best approach," and quite another thing to say, "The inductive arguments for the existence of God are to be totally abandoned." When the theistic apriorist takes the position that if anyone denies the triune, sovereign God, it is of no value to present the theistic evidence, he is setting up an unnecessary barrier to a multitude of bewildered people.

C. *The Rationalistic A Priori*

There are devout Christian scholars of the present generation who hold to an inflexible deductive rationalism. It is their thought that by rigid adherence to laws of logic (as they conceive the laws of logic) the existence of God, the authority of the Bible, and thus the entire Christian system of doctrine, can be deduced. I know a Christian scholar of considerable influence who holds to this type of rationalism, if I understand him correctly, and I think I do. For him the Anselmic deductive ontological argument is the only argument for the existence of God which has any validity. He holds that God cannot be known by His works, that arguments from the cosmos or any part of the cosmos, as an effect, to God as Cause, is invalid argument. He even goes so far as to say that such processes cannot correctly be called arguments! He sometimes speaks as though the only logic is the logic of a deductive syllogism the premises of which are rational axioms.

He carries his rationalistic apriorism to such extremes that he argues that scientific inductive processes cannot attain any truth. Scientific statements about matters of material fact, such as the time of sunset, and the time of the tides, he will not admit are true statements, even within the horizon of discourse in which they are given. "No," says he, "they are all false statements, however useful they may be."

From the statement that the truth as a whole is a perfectly integrated consistent system, including all of reality, he sometimes argues in published statements that "system," that is, the word itself, means "perfectly consistent, integrated totality." This view was advocated by Kierkegaard in his arguments against Hegel's philosophy. It is denied that the word "system" could ever apply to a complex of principles in the least degree inconsistent or lacking in total comprehensiveness.[6]

The rationalistic *a priori* method is exemplified in Professor Hackett's new book, *The Resurrection of Theism*.[7] Hackett holds to an elaborate system of logical principles and categories based upon a modification of Kant's system of pure reason. He believes that by the application of these logical principles and categories the existence of God can be conclusively demonstrated, and so, the truths of the Bible can be established.

With all respect to the laws and categories of logic, I must say that no human being could know the existence of God by mere logical principles. The God of the Judeo-Christian tradition is an existing Personal Spirit, a substantive entity, with certain specifiable attributes. He has given factual revelation of Himself in human experience. I believe that Moses and the prophets, and supremely Jesus Christ, are actual historical characters, and that what the Bible says about them, and through them, is verifiably true. I believe that in the experience of Moses and the prophets, God spoke, and that in the person of Jesus Christ God spoke in the flesh. The divine revelation set forth in the Bible was given in terms of time and place and linguistic communication. I believe that to understand this revelation we must apply the established rules of grammatico-historical exegesis. I believe that all that is contained in the Christian revelation is reasonable. Nothing violates the principles of logic. We do not believe contradic-

[6]For what I consider the proper usage of the word "system," see *A Christian View of Men and Things* by Gordon H. Clark, Eerdmans, 1952: "But suppose there still remain two or more fairly self-consistent but mutually incompatible systems of thought. This is likely to be the case. . . . Instead of being thoroughly integrated, the opposing systems will lack some parts and connections." (p. 32) "No philosopher is perfect and no system can give man omniscience. But if one system can provide plausible solutions to many problems while another [system] leaves too many questions unanswered, if one system tends less to skepticism and gives more meaning to life. . . ." (p. 34) "Even systems of philosophy, like neo-scholasticism . . . must still meet the most serious objections to their views in the field of epistemology." (p. 285)
[7]Professor Hackett is a devout Christian scholar of outstanding ability. I much regret that in my review of this book in *Christianity Today*, the editor, without my knowledge, cut out certain favorable comments of mine.

tory propositions. But factual existences never can be deduced from mere abstract logical principles. God has spoken!

D. *Have We "Common Ground"?*

Influential Christian scholars in our generation are teaching that since man exists in a fallen condition, and since his mind is distorted by sin, there is no common ground, in reason or in evidences, between the Christian and his message, on the one hand, and the unbeliever on the other. This view has been called "presuppositionalism," not because those who oppose it do not frankly state their presuppositions, but because, according to this particular *a priori* view, there is no intellectual common ground *unless* one adopts distinctly Christian presuppositions.

Those who hold to this type of apriorism analyze the state of mind of the unbeliever as though he were completely committed to a fully elaborated, totally anti-theistic view of the universe. The Christian believes that God is the Creator of all the objects of nature. The unbeliever is supposed to be explicitly committed to the position that there is no Creator of nature. Now since God is the Creator, the unbeliever cannot know the things of nature in any degree of truthfulness. The Christian and the unbeliever, it is argued, both drink milk from a red cow; but the unbeliever, since he denies that God is the Creator of red cows, cannot even know a red cow. All of his opinions are false because they all supposedly include the logically elaborated dogma that God is not the Creator and that man is self-sufficient in his own rational powers.

Fortunately, this type of presuppositionalism is never consistently carried out. In discussion with scholars of this type I have sometimes said, "But I am acquainted with many unbelievers, whom I have met in pastoral experience, who are not committed to any anti-theistic philosophy, least of all to an elaborated anti-theistic view. I know many unbelievers who are simply lost, bewildered, and in the dark."

The reply has usually been, "Why certainly that is true. We are only speaking of the logical implications." Yet the teaching goes on, and many young men have been impressed with the idea that it is improper to present evidences and reasons to the unsaved man.

This position is taken to such extremes that the historical inductive arguments for the existence of God are said to be not only false but harmful. As one of the presuppositionalists puts it, "Whereas Professor Hepp [of Amsterdam] says that the cosmological and teleological arguments cry out day and night to the glory of God, as a matter of fact the cosmological and teleological arguments cry out day and night 'there is no God!' "[8]

E. *Calvin and Pre-suppositionalism*

The doctrine which we have called "presuppositionalism" is alleged to be "Calvinistic." On the contrary, a careful study of Calvin's writings will show that the presuppositionalist position is not the position which he holds. It is in Book II, Chapter II of the *Institutes* that Calvin gives the most extended discussion of the psychology of fallen man. In paragraph 12 he says, "For although we [i.e. humanity in the lost condition] retain some portion of understanding and judgment together with the will, yet we cannot say that our mind is perfect and sound, which is oppressed with debility and immersed in profound darkness. . . . Reason, therefore, by which man distinguishes between good and evil, by which he understands and judges, being a natural talent, could not be totally destroyed, but is partly debilitated, partly vitiated . . . some sparks continue to shine in the nature of man, even in its corrupt and degenerate state, which prove him to be a rational creature, different from the brute, because he is endued with understanding . . . let us first examine the power of the understanding. To condemn it to perpetual blindness, so as to leave it no intelligence in anything, is repugnant, not only to the divine work, but also to the experience of common sense."

At the end of paragraph thirteen Calvin says, "Yet it is certainly true, that some seeds of political order are sown in the minds of all. And this is a powerful argument, that in

[8]Cf. Cornelius Van Til *Common Grace* 1947, Presb. and Ref. Pub. Co., p. 61.

the constitution of this life no man is destitute of the light of reason." This chapter of the *Institutes* has many such statements. In the last paragraph of Book II, Chapter VI, with reference to fallen man, Calvin says, "I grant that he has a mind capable of understanding, though it attains not to heavenly and spiritual wisdom; he has some idea of virtue; he has some sense of the Deity, though he acquires not the true knowledge of God."

Calvin's constant assumption, like the assumption of the writers of the Scriptures, is that fallen man may hear and understand something of the Word of God and may, by the convicting power of the Holy Spirit, be convinced, and believe. This is the assumption of Christ in dealing with even the most perverse of men. "Ye hypocrites, *ye can discern* the face of the sky and of the earth; but how is it that ye do not discern this time? Yea, and why even of yourselves judge ye not what is right?" (Luke 12:56, 57)

Conclusion

I would urge then that the types of apriorism discussed in this chapter be rejected, not in their affirmative assumptions, but in their negative attitude toward such broken fragments of the truth as may be found in the minds of ignorant or wayward men. I would urge the use of the inductive processes[9] of presenting evidence, not as the only method, but as a method of pointing to the truth useful and profitable in many situations.

[9]Detailed study of inductive reasoning processes cannot be included in the present work, but is covered in a course in logic. The student should read the article on "Reasoning" by C. S. Peirce in Baldwin's *Dictionary* (Vol. II, pp. 426 ff.).

Note: A new introduction to the Amsterdam philosophy of *Witsidee,* or philosophy of Cosmonomic Idea, has come to my desk since the completion of my work on the page proofs of this text. It is Professor Dooyeweerd's *Twilight of Western Thought*, Grand Rapids, Baker Book House, 1960. Dooyeweerd's is an *a priori* Christian philosophy. I have sincere respect for the scholars who adhere to this view in Holland and America, but I am not convinced that they have, as yet, produced a great Biblical system of philosophical thought.

Chapter VIII

CONSTRUCTIVE SUGGESTIONS

A. *Dualism in Epistemology*

Dualistic realism is a term which applies primarily to metaphysics, but it implies a dualistic epistemology. If we accept the theory that there are two kinds of substantive entities, extended things and thinking things, some knowledge of extended things which do not think, is implied. Therefore, necessarily there must be some degree of dualism in the knowledge process.

However, the dualism of epistemology is not identical with the dualism of ontology. The dualism of epistemology involves the distinction between the thinking *subject*, and the matter thought about, which is usually called the *object* of thought. The object of thought may be another mind or spirit, or the thinker himself, or some phase of the thinker's mental experience. Thus, while the *subject* of epistemology is always within the class of thinking things of ontology, the *object* of epistemology may not be within the class of extended things of ontology. The object includes, of course, all extended things of which we have any knowledge, but it also includes any and all thinking things and their experiences, insofar as these are ever thought about.

B. *Overlapping of Metaphysics*

The fact that metaphysics and epistemology overlap, is indicated in the last section above, and also in many other portions of this study. Many aspects of epistemology have necessarily been touched upon throughout the chapters of Part I and Part II. In discussing what we believe to exist, it is inevitable that we say something about our reasons for believing as we do. As indicated above, Professor James Iverach in his excellent article on "Epistemology" points out that epistemology grows out of metaphysics and is secondary thereto. There will therefore be some repetition as, from the point of view of epistemology, we discuss our reasons for believing. Believing is now the matter of primary interest; the substance of what we believe is background material.

Epistemology is a vast field including not only our reasons for holding to our view of metaphysics, but also including our reasons for holding to the abstract principles of logic and mathematics, which constitute sub-departments in the general field of epistemology itself.

C. *Intuitive Knowledge*

It is generally agreed in all kinds of theories of knowledge that we do have some immediate experiences which are given without the involvement of any reasoning process, without any presenting of evidence or drawing of inferences. A common illustration of such experiences is the observation of the color of a dandelion. The word "intuition" comes from the Latin word *intuere,* which means simply "to look at." We find *given* in our experience the color of the dandelion. There it is and there is no arguing about it. If anyone else does not see it, if it is not given in his experience, we are not responsible for that. For us it is immediate intuitive data.

From this point on I find myself quite radically diverging from the major part of the literature on this subject. I have not been able to find any study in the field of epistemology which has applied the principles developed in *Gestalt* psychology, though, with the enormous mass of written material in this field, it would not be surprising if such a work has appeared without my knowledge.[1]

Students of the overlapping fields of psychology and epis-

[1]Although Professor Iverach wrote his article on "Epistemology," referred to above, before *Gestalt* psychology came into prominence, he anticipates many of its findings. For him intuitive experience is the experience of dynamic situations, and not primarily the experience of the dismembered parts of *Gestalten.* The German word *Gestalt* is not easy to translate. "Configuration" is the word used most often in works on psychology. *Gestalt* psychology emphasizes the fact that we naturally experience things as dynamic wholes.

temology, from William James[2] on down to recent times, have examined intuitive knowledge by a process of detailed analysis. First, they say, we are conscious of a mere sensation. After this first step the writers in the field do not agree in their processes of analysis, but there is partial unanimity in the following rough outline:

(2) We are conscious of our consciousness of sensation. It is sometimes said that an animal does not think about his mental experiences as we do. Kipling somewhere suggests that elephants "look inside their heads" or, in other words, reflect about their own thoughts. This second step is something of a side step leading to the examination of the thinker. In many systems what I call step number three is designated as step number two.

(3) Perception follows sensation. After the mere sensation of the color of the dandelion, in our consciousness we say there it is out there. In other words, we interpret the sensation as having reference to an object.

(4) Concept follows perception. We conceive of the object as being a dandelion growing in the grass.

(5) Judgment follows concept. We reflect, "The dandelion ought not to be there. If I had enough gumption I'd dig it out, but probably I won't."

Now all of this is interesting analysis, but, in my judgment, it does not correspond to fact. It is more like an ancient method of teaching a foreign language by first memorizing a vast amount of grammatical data, conjugations, declensions, rules, vocabulary, and then, after a while, beginning to read a few sentences. That simply is not the way human beings learn to talk. Meaningful words and combinations of words come first. Afterwards (and, we regret to say, in the education of many of our young people, never) comes the knowledge of grammatical and syntactical principles.

Similarly I would strongly urge that the elementary units

[2]The "steps" in the process of intuitive knowledge may of course be traced far beyond William James. The roots of the analysis are in Kant, Hume, Berkeley, Locke and so on back. In the recent past F. R. Tennant's "genetic psychology" (Vol. I of his *Philosophical Theology*) carries out the analysis to the nth degree.

of intuitive experience are *Gestalten,* dynamic configurations. A child learns what a chair is long before he learns to observe and analyze the structural parts of a chair. I do not believe that anyone in intuitive experience goes through the steps which the atomistic psychological epistemologists have elaborated. Nobody says to himself (1) I have a sensation of yellow; (2) I am conscious of it as a sensation; (3) I perceive a yellow object; (4) I form the conception of a dandelion out there in the grass; (5) I must do something about it. No; all of these aspects of experience come at once as a dynamic whole.

It may be argued that I am not pointing out an elementary unit of intuitive experience, but rather a mature experience which has involved a long process of the formation of habits of thought. I do not believe this criticism is valid. Granted that there are some people who have not previously experienced a dandelion in the grass. Even for such, I insist, the elementary experience is, "there is a yellow object out there." Certainly there are many human beings for whom the judgment, the step which I have numbered five, would be different. A dandelion in itself is beautiful and attractive. For a child the primary impulse seems to be, "Let me go and pick it." The judgment, "I should dig it out," is of course a product of culture.

Nevertheless, in spite of flaws in my presentation, I believe it is important for us to realize that our elementary intuitive experiences are dynamic situations and not mere sensations.

Someone will object that surely step number five is not a part of an elementary intuitive experience. Many experiences come to us without resulting in any form of judgment. This opinion I believe is mistaken. Iverach points out that our experiences are selective, and since they are selective, they are teleological, they involve purpose. Those events in our surroundings which do not in some way lead to our taking an attitude, or passing a simple judgment, are not really experiences. Some years ago I read of an entomologist and a bank clerk who were walking through Times Square at the noon hour.

The sidewalks were crowded with people and many were walking in the streets. The street cars (this was years ago) were loudly banging over their intersections. Buses and trucks were competing with taxicabs and private cars for every inch of forward moving space. Suddenly the entomologist stopped and exclaimed, "I hear a cricket." The bank clerk heard nothing. The entomologist stepped to the curb, looked around carefully, and found the cricket in his strange surroundings.

"How could you possibly have heard that cricket with all the noise and bustle about us?" inquired the bank clerk.

"That's easy," said the entomologist, "I am an entomologist. I am interested in such things."

The bank clerk was still incredulous.

"People hear what they are interested in," said the entomologist. "Now look." He took a thin dime from his pocket and dropped it on the concrete sidewalk. All the scurrying people within a hundred feet paused for a moment and turned their heads. The sound of the dime was not nearly as loud as the sound of the cricket, but they were interested in dimes. Few were interested in crickets. The sound of the cricket simply was not an experience for them, but the sound of a dime dropping on the concrete walk was a dynamic situation.

Not sensations, but *Gestalten,* are elementary intuitive experiences; but this must not be understood by the student as implying that these dynamic configurations or situations are unanalyzable. Even the atomistic epistemologists, who have begun with mere sensations, have not made so bold as to assert that what they took to be elementary, as given in experience, is necessarily incapable of analysis in the ontological world. Sensations themselves were analyzed; and *Gestalten* certainly should be analyzed. What I insist upon is that the various aspects of our intuitive experiences should be recognized for what they are.

Elementary intuitive experiences always involve *all the major categories* of the dualistic realistic view. The categories are there as unanalyzed, or even unconscious, assumptions. The fact that they are given in intuitive experience explains the fact that they are found in discourse.[3] Our elementary intuitive experiences are of the pattern, "I see a dandelion out there in the grass." The intuition itself, the given in consciousness includes the subject, the object, the substance, the attributes, the space, the time, the valuation and the setting in the stream of causality.

It may seem that we are driving toward an extreme form of naive realism, which is accused of saying, "The dandelion is in my mind; my mind has gone out to embrace it and to include it." No. Naive people know the difference between seeing a thing, and getting it in the eye! The accusation of so-called naive realism (and I do not think naive people really hold the absurd opinions ascribed to them by the neo-realists and the critical realists) cannot be laid to the door of the dualistic realist in his dualistic epistemology. The *Gestalt* is given as a whole with all of its parts dynamically integrated in immediate intuitive experience.

But the *Gestalt* must now be analyzed. Perhaps a dandelion is an hallucination. Perhaps I am dreaming. Perhaps I have indigestion and lights are floating before my eyes where no lights ought to be. An immediate intuitive experience is not a substantive entity. It may be a part of reality simply in the category of mental images. The analysis must proceed if we are to come to any solid basis for knowledge.

I look steadily at the dandelion. It does not disappear or jump around or become a dozen dandelions. If it did I should be alarmed. I take the dandelion in experience as a signal *of something* in the world of substantive entities. I do not by any means assume that the something of which the experience is a signal, is necessarily like the signal itself. Suppose I walk out onto the grass and the dandelion jumps around as I turn my eyes. My conclusion is that the something in the world of substantive entities must have been like a glimpse of the sun, or a flash bulb going off within my field of vision. On the other hand, if the dandelion becomes a dozen bright spots

---

[3]I have elsewhere discussed the elaborate epistemology of F. R. Tennant. He is definitely atomistic in his methods. However, he points out the significant fact that no one can consistently deny that so-called knowledge takes place — so-called knowledge by a so-called subject of a so-called object.

floating slowly about, my conclusion is that the something in the realm of substantive entities is in the nature of indigestion, or abnormal blood pressure. I must see a doctor.

If, as I approach the dandelion and bring it near to my eye, its outlines become indistinct and blurred, I do not ascribe the fact to any change in the dandelion as a substantive entity, but the cause which I infer is the fact that I have gone out without my trifocals.

To summarize the matter of intuitive experience, it is the contention of dualistic realism, that elementary intuitive experiences imply, consciously or unconsciously, all the major categories which are to be found in human discourse. These elementary intuitive experiences, when further analyzed, should be regarded as signals caused by objects which may or may not be quite dissimilar to the signals which they cause.

D. *The Order of Nature*[4]

Pursuant to the analysis of elementary intuitive experiences, the next major step in epistemology may properly be an inquiry as to the relation of our knowledge to the kind of world of which these experiences may be considered to be signals.

It is my suggestion that elementary intuitive experiences lead to the theory that there are ontologically existing substantive entities which occupy space, entities with which we have to do. At the same time elementary intuitive experiences lead to the inference that there are thinking beings with whom we have to do, and who, like ourselves, have to do with each other and with extended things in the world. It is my opinion that our process of coming to believe in ourselves as thinking beings, and in others as thinking beings, is implied in the elementary intuitive experience, and is developed by a process of inference from effects to causes. I have not held that elementary intuitive experiences give immediate knowledge of any substantive entity whatsoever. These experiences take place as dynamic situations, or *Gestalten*. They appear as

---

[4]Normally, for children in a Christian home, knowledge of God in Christ should come early in the process of knowledge of other objective reality, and should develop and permeate and integrate with the total human experience.

184

signals caused by substantive entities. What I am arguing is that the idea of thinking things and extended things interacting, is a part of our elementary intuitive experiences. From there on, the process is one of *inference* from effects to causes. We trace the natural development of our thinking, as it begins with elementary intuitive experiences, and from such experiences, as a further step, to the postulation of the order of nature.

E. *The Order of Valid Thought*

In the history of human culture, and I believe in the natural development of the individual mind, reflection upon the validity of thought comes after the exercise of more or less valid thinking with reference to elementary intuitive experiences and the order of nature. Logic was not formally developed until Aristotle, but the laws of logic were assumed in ancient Semitic literature long before the time of Aristotle.

(1) The Law of Contradictories

Although I hold that logic is a subdivision of epistemology, yet, since logic is usually offered as a separate course, and is usually written about in separate treatises, this obviously is not the place for anything like a full development of the principles of logic. Only a few suggestions in outline are in order.

The principle of logic most obvious to the ordinary mind, and most easily grasped, is the principle that contradictory statements cannot both be true. A distinction between truth and falsehood, and strong opposition to a lie are matters of great emphasis in the ancient Hebrew Scriptures. The law of contradictories was assumed and taken for granted many centuries before the formulation of logical principles by Aristotle.

The relationship of contradictory propositions is illustrated by the diagonal lines in the diagram on the following page. The four types of propositions illustrated in the diagram are traditionally designated by the first four vowels, AEIO. An A proposition is a universal affirmative: "All A is B." An E proposition is a universal negative: "No A is B." An I propo-

"THE SQUARE OF OPPOSITION"

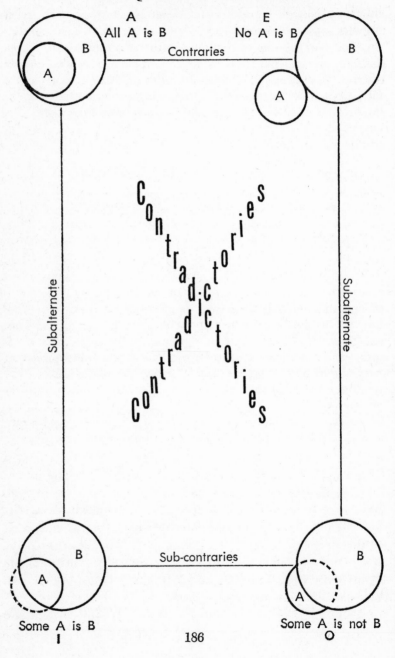

sition is a particular affirmative: "Some A is B." An O proposition is a particular negative: "Some A is not B."

For our present purpose the most important lines in the diagram are the diagonals. These point to contradictory propositions. According to the law of contradictories, if all A is B (if all cows are quadrupeds) the statement that some A is not B (that some cows are not quadrupeds) must be false, and vice versa. A similar relationship obtains between an E proposition and an I proposition.

Other lines in the diagram are not as important as the contradictories for our purposes. Obviously contraries are also contradictories. Sub-contraries may or may not be contradictories. An I proposition and an O proposition, using the same terms of course, may both be true, may both be false, or either one may be true and the other false. The term subalternate refers to an I proposition with reference to an A proposition, or to an O proposition with reference to an E proposition. In cases where the terms of an A or an E proposition refer to known substantive entities, if the A or E proposition is true, the corresponding subalternate will also be true. If all cows eat grass it follows that some cows eat grass. However, if the terms of an A or an E proposition refer to non-existent imaginary beings, the corresponding subalternate propositions would be false. We may say "all centaurs eat grass." This could be taken as true in the sense that all the centaurs that exist, that is none at all, eat grass. But the subalternate proposition would not be true for when we say, "some centaurs eat grass," the word "some" implies existing substantive entities, and there are none.

(2) The Law of Identity

More fundamental than the law of contradictories, but less obvious, less transparent, are the laws of identity and excluded middle. These laws are equally fundamental to all reasonable discourse prior to the discovery of the laws of logic by Aristotle, but it is not so easy to cause the ordinary mind to focus upon them.

The law of identity says, "A is A." What this means is

simply that, in reasonable discourse, terms may be identified as having a fixed meaning within a given context. This does not deny that, if terms designate substantive entities, the entities themselves may be subject to constant change. If one should say "four pecks make a bushel" this would be a statement of abstract relationships in space; but if one should say "this peck of potatoes was purchased at the store," the term "this peck of potatoes" can logically be taken as a fixed term of discourse, regardless of the fact that before the discourse comes to an end, the potatoes may have disappeared entirely or in part.

In other words, the law of identity means that we can know what we are talking about in spite of the fact that the world of substantive entities is constantly in a process of change.

(3) The Law of Excluded Middle

The law of excluded middle is still more difficult to explain and to illustrate. It is traditionally stated, "A is either B or non-B." This does not mean of course that a potato cannot be partly good and partly bad. What it really means is that in discourse where the terms are clearly defined and unambiguous, propositions with reference to the inclusion or exclusion of terms in classes, are either true or false. This assumption is the basis of what is called a two-valued logic — clear-cut properly constructed propositions are either true or false.[5]

I have stated the law of contradictories first because it is most easily understood. After all three are understood, it is apparent that the law of identity should come first. In logical thinking it is first necessary that we should know the terms about which we are speaking before we can make statements about propositions including terms. In traditional logic, therefore, the three laws are given in this order: the law of identity;

[5]Two-valued logic is not contrary to multi-valued logic, if properly understood. In two-valued logic we assume that the truth or falsehood of propositions is either known or knowable. In multi-valued logic we assume that we do not know whether the propositions are true or false. Multi-valued logic calculates the probability of the truth or falsehood of propositions, the truth or falsity of which is assumed to be unknown.

the law of contradiction; the law of excluded middle. To use the alphabetical formula, A is A; A is not non-A; A is either B or non-B.

(4) The Laws of Reason Taken Together

Similar to the basic laws of logic are the basic laws of mathematics. Arithmetic, algebra and Euclidian geometry are based upon certain so-called axioms, or primary truths, sometimes called self-evident truths, which need not here be elaborated, because they are so well known.

Taken together, the laws of logic and the laws of mathematics may be called the laws of reason, or the laws of valid thinking.

(5) Criteria of the Laws of Reason

The laws of valid thinking are an essential part of epistemology, but epistomology has not performed its essential task inside of the scope of these laws. Epistemology must also stand outside and say, "What is the basis of these laws and how do we know that they are to be accepted?"

(a) John Dewey's view

I have discussed at length elsewhere the logic of John Dewey and the instrumentalists, commonly called pragmatists. Briefly, the pragmatic criterion is the solution of problems for the time being. It is Dewey's view that the laws of logic and of mathematics are not eternal immutable principles of reason, but are products of the social inquiry process. There is abroad a popular notion to the effect that Einstein's theory of relativity destroyed the previously assumed validity of mathematical laws and therefore destroyed the permanent validity of the basic laws of reason. Many have gone so far as to use mathematical relativity as an excuse for giving up the Ten Commandments and all the essential principles of truth and ethics. This error is, in large part, traceable to Dewey's enormous influence. In discussing Dewey's epistemology[6] I have shown that the great authority on the mathematics of relativity, Albert Einstein, has explicitly declared that his sys-

[6]*Philosophies of F. R. Tennant and John Dewey*, chapter on Dewey's epistemology.

tem of mathematics is not at all contrary to the logic of Euclidean geometry. It is based on somewhat different definitions, and it takes into account more complicated situations in the physical world. But the laws of Euclid are perfectly logical and have not been repealed or modified. "Relativity" in logic and ethics, abandoning the eternal verities, has no basis in genuine science or mathematics. I do not know who said it first, but it is a saying worth emphatic repetiton, "Whoever seeks to destroy the laws of logic, logic destroys him." The pragmatic criterion must be rejected.

(b) The Apriorists

Charles Hodge and Robert Flint and many of the theologians of the nineteenth century frequently spoke of "self-evident truths." The laws of reason were taken to be, as the German says, *selbstandig*. They are given and there is no possibility of examining their foundations, since they are the foundation of all rational thought, for which there could be no criterion.

Some of the older apriorists did, in a way, seek to examine the foundations of these "self-evident" principles. It was suggested by some that these are "innate ideas" or that they are put into the constitution of the mind by the Creator, in such a way that all minds are compelled to think in accordance with them. The fact that some minds do not think in accordance with these principles, or do not always so think, was of course observed, but it was thought that irrational minds were either abnormal, disorganized or malicious.

(c) The Arbitrary View

There are among our contemporaries in the mid-twentieth century certain influential individuals who hold that the laws of reason are *created* by the arbitrary will of God, in such a sense that God could have made multiplication tables with meanings directly contradictory to the meanings which are now set forth in these tables.

It is even suggested that we can now, with our present mentality, speak intelligibly in terms which contradict what are usually called the basic laws of reason. It is held that the question:

> "If one third of six is three,
> What will one fourth of twenty be?"

is capable of a rational answer.

The equations used are as follows:

$$\tfrac{1}{3} \times 6 \times X = 3$$
$$2X = 3$$
$$X = 1\tfrac{1}{2}$$
$$\tfrac{1}{4} \times 20 \times 1\tfrac{1}{2} = 7\tfrac{1}{2}$$

But I argue that the first equation in the series is not a proper statement of the question in the quoted rhyme. The equation with which the series begins is a statement of the question, "If in calculating one third of six with an error, the result, three, is obtained, assuming then the same rate of error, what will one fourth of twenty be?"

Literally taking the question as given in the rhyme, the first equation would have to be:

$$\tfrac{6}{3} = 3$$
$$\text{Then, } 2 = 3$$
$$0 = 1$$

Taking the first equation and canceling out the fraction, two equals three. Subtracting from each side of the equation, zero equals one. Now if zero equals one, all discourse is at an end. Nothing means anything.

Another way of taking the question literally would be:

$$\tfrac{6}{3} = 3$$
$$6 = 9, \text{ etc.}$$

The fact that all meaning is gone if the laws of reason are denied, is not apparent to all.[7] One of our prominent contemporaries is emphatic in his rejection of the law of contradictories. He declares that Christians must believe the doctrine of the Trinity as a paradox in the modern dialectical sense.

[7]Note that the question does not concern the mere mark by which we designate the concept "three." No one denies that the mark "3" might have stood for the concept which we now call "two."

The view that the Trinity, though a mystery, is not a contradiction, is regarded by him with suspicion. He says in no uncertain terms that the doctrine of the Trinity is a formal contradiction in terms of Aristotle's logic. This is not the statement of a liberal. Fosdick is quoted as saying that the doctrine of the Trinity is a contradiction in arithmetic. But I am referring to the statement of a Biblical, theistic, apriorist, who demands that we must believe the doctrine of the Trinity as a doctrine which is contrary to the laws of reason.[8]

Regardless of the approach to the question, there are, fortunately, few Bible-believing theologians who take the position (advanced by Kierkegaard and Barth) that we must believe "a paradox" in the sense of a formal contradiction.

(d) Integration

For the majority of philosophers, Christian and non-Christian alike, the law of contradictories is accepted as the chief law of reason, and the criterion of the laws of reason is expressed in terms such as "coherence," "consistency," "correspondence." Coherence and consistency, as I see it, are practically synonymous. They are equivalent to a restatement of the law of contradictories.

It is true that some have taken the criterion of coherence or consistency as an affirmative criterion. It has been held that whatever is coherent or consistent may be taken as true. Such a position is of course unfortunate and leads to absurdities. It might be quite consistent and quite coherent for a dairyman to believe that the moon is a great round cheese. There have been people who were sure of it. They could see that a dragon ate it up once a month and it was subsequently replaced month by month. With limited information (and all human information is limited) coherence and consistency may characterize theories which later prove to be absurdities.

Coherence and consistency are reliable criteria if taken in a merely negative sense. That which is not coherent and

[8] The revealed Triune character of God is indeed a mystery, but it is *not* a formal contradiction.

which is not consistent involves some falsehood somewhere, and should be rejected until the falsehood is located and coherence or consistency restored.

Correspondence is a term, based upon the law of contradictories, which applies to *propositional* truths. A proposition may be taken as true if it corresponds to the ontological situation, as evidenced through an experimental process called verification. The correspondence criterion is also merely negative, when properly employed.

As a matter of terminology, I prefer the word "integration" to designate the criterion of the laws of reason, chiefly of the law of contradictories. This word integration implies, I think, a little more than negative non-contradiction. It is not merely a restatement of that of which it is the criterion. The truth will not only be consistent and coherent, and propositions will not only correspond to the results of verification, but truths when ascertained will be found to work together and supplement one another in an integrated system as a whole.

(6) The Source of the Laws of Reason

We have not yet given a positive answer to the question of the source of the laws of reason. Are these laws "self evident" in the sense that they contain their own verification? Are they "innate ideas" in the sense that our minds are so constituted that we cannot think otherwise, even though we might postulate other minds for whom the laws of reason would not be valid? Is the question as to the source or ground of the laws of reason unanswerable? Or perhaps even unaskable?

As for myself, I believe that the question is askable, that is, the question has an intelligible meaning to the ordinary mind; and I believe the question is also answerable. I should like to make two suggestions: First, I believe that the laws of reason are derived from the character of God. I have already pointed out that the writers of the Bible constantly assume and frequently assert that it is impossible for God to lie. I have shown that their meaning is not the mere tautology that whatever God might say would be true because He said it. The

193

meaning is that mere human beings may count upon the consistency, the coherence, the correspondence, the integration of whatever God has said, integration with ontological reality, and with whatever God may say in the future. My reasons for believing that the laws of reason are derived from the character of God involve all the reasons for my acceptance of the Christian system of doctrine and life. Elaboration of these reasons would constitute a full course in apologetics.

Second, I suggest that the laws of reason are discoverable by experience, experience including revelation and the evidences for revelation.

I hesitate to use the term "empirical basis," for I do not regard the empirical process as an ultimate basis. The suggestion that the laws of reason are obtained by and in the process of experience is somewhat radical and revolutionary but I do believe that this is the case.

I hasten to say that I thoroughly reject John Dewey's contention, which he makes throughout his *Logic,* that the laws of logic are *produced by* the inquiry process itself and are not *a priori truth.* I have shown that Dewey misquotes and misinterprets Peirce on the subject. I believe, as Peirce believed, that the laws of reason are eternal verities, but that they are *discovered* empirically.

F. *Faith as a Principle of Reason*

The small boy in Sunday school explained to the teacher, "Faith is tryin' awful hard to believe sumpin' that really ain't so except on Sunday!" It is not at all uncommon, if faith is mentioned in a work of philosophy, to find that it is assumed to be opposed to reason, or at least quite beyond and outside of the area of reasonable evidence. On the contrary, faith should be defined as the wholehearted acceptance of conclusions for which there is good and sufficient evidence.[9]

This definition of faith includes both an objective and a subjective reference. In some contexts the word "faith" primarily refers to *what* we believe. In other contexts the primary

[9]See my article, "The Ethics of Pisteuo in the Fourth Gospel," in the *Bibliotheca Sacra* for January, 1923, Volume LXXX, No. 317.

reference is to the *act* of believing. It is my opinion that in every instance of the proper usage of the word faith, both the objective and the subjective side of faith are included, but the emphasis differs.

For the objective meaning of faith take I John 5:4, "This is the victory which overcometh the world, even our faith." It is the objective meaning which is prominent all through the eleventh chapter of the Epistle to the Hebrews. It is what we believe, as centered in the finished work of Christ, which constitutes the "substance" of things hoped for and the "evidence" of things not as yet seen. What we already believe is essential to what we expect to observe in the future.

The relationship between faith and understanding is suggested in Hebrews 11:3, "Through faith we understand. . . ." These are strange words if we are to define faith as opposed to reason. But with the definition given above, this verse is not only intelligible but wonderfully illuminating. "By faith we understand that the worlds were made (set in order) by the word of God, so that what we look at has not come into being from phenomenological objects."[10] In other words, what we believe, as centered in the finished work of Christ, makes the theistic doctrine of creation intelligible.

Paul's word to the Philippian jailer (Acts 16:31) "Believe on the Lord Jesus Christ, and thou shalt be saved, and thy house," emphasized the subjective aspect of faith. It is assumed that the jailer had heard the "good news," and understood the factual content of the story of Jesus. Instead of committing suicide, as he was about to do, he was invited to believe, trust, put his confidence in the crucified risen Saviour. In other words, he was called upon to *accept* an intelligible interpretation of things, based upon the data which he had observed.

Note the intellectual problem of the jailer at this point. If the prisoners had escaped, he would be executed for betrayal of his trust. Now, however, though the doors were open and the stocks were broken by the earthquake, the prisoners had not escaped. All reason for suicide was gone.

[10]My translation.

What did the jailer mean by his reference to salvation? The only answer is that, the physical danger of being executed for the loss of the prisoners now totally removed, he must have been concerned about spiritual things. He must have heard enough of the testimony of Paul and Silas to have asked his question with specific spiritual reference. He was called upon to accept Christ as his personal Saviour. He knew the facts. He was called upon for a decision, an act of the will, a commitment.

The philosopher Nietzsche (1844-1900) in his *Ecce Homo* says, "In the end, nobody hears more out of things, including books, than he knows already. For that to which one lacks access from experience, one has no ears."[11] This statement is of course exaggerated, but it points to an important truth, namely that our elementary intuitive experiences are selective. This has been discussed in part in the above section on intuitive knowledge. It was there indicated that our elementary intuitive experiences are *Gestalten,* or dynamic configurations, or situations in which intuition gives may elements, including causal relationships, and the distinction between subject and object. The *Gestalten* which come into our experience are selected. Iverach, in the article on epistemology above referred to, points out that "knowledge is teleological." In the fact that we select what we see and what we hear, we *choose* what we experience. The focus of our eyes, the attention of our hearing, the reaching of our hands, all are selective and volitional. Though the voluntary aspect of intuitive experiences is often habitual and unconscious, nevertheless the volitional factor is definitely a part of intuitive experiences.

We must now emphasize the fact that not only in intuitive experiences, but in the entire learning process, volition is a real factor. It has been explained above that faith includes both the objective and the subjective. Faith includes what we believe and the act of believing. It has also been

[11]Quoted in *Existentialism from Dostoevsky to Sartre,* compiled by Walter Kaufmann, Meridian, 1956, p. 111.

indicated that the act of believing is in a large measure dependent upon, and influenced by, what we already believe.

We stand again at a point at which our ontology and epistemology cannot be separated. The nature of our ontology is closely integrated with the nature of our epistemology. If we do not believe in the reality of the world of material and spiritual substantive entities, we might go on to a subjective idealistic interpretation. If believing is a process of selecting voluntarily and accepting only what we already believe, as Nietzsche suggests, we might as well be pure subjectivists or even Christian Scientists. We might as well define as true whatever we wish to believe. Since everyone creates his own universe according to his own liking we might as well quit studying philosophy or anything else. In fact, nothing *matters,* so never *mind!*

For the dualistic realist, subjectivism is impossible. Ontological truth is there to be discovered whether we discover it or not. We frankly and even gladly accept what Tennant[12] calls "the volitional elements in the unification of experience." What we believe depends in large part upon what we have already accepted as true. What we believe also depends upon our willingness to believe.[13] But the dualistic realist believes in the interaction between his mind and the ontological world of substantive entities. If the world is real, and if the so-called laws of reason are true, it would follow that experience of reality would lead to a larger and larger integration as experience increases. It would also follow that erroneous opinions previously held, and erroneous judgments, accepting as truths propositions which do not correspond to reality, would lead to greater and greater frustration with less and less genuine integration.

It is observable in psychology that our elementary intuitive experiences are subject to correction. What we take for

[12]See Tennant's article on causality in E. R. E. above referred to.
[13]The student may ask how it is possible for a child to begin the knowledge process. Our point of discussion here is the theory of knowledge, not the psychology of the beginning of knowledge. However, it should not be difficult to understand the beginnings of the knowledge process in the experience of a child through the operation of instinct, or inborn behavior tendencies.

genuine *Gestalten* in reality may be illusions or hallucinations. Or the genuine *Gestalten* experienced in immaturity may prove to be dynamic parts of larger configurations. It is this latter process which generally characterizes mature thinking. We do not abandon previously discovered truths, but we see such truths in larger and larger relationships.

I believe from experience with children, that chronologically in the development of a child, faith in God should be expected to develop at an early age. Probably it is preceded by the act of faith in parents and faith in outward reality. It hardly seems possible that faith in the laws of reason would become explicit at an early age. Most children have to learn the difference between truth and falsehood by severe experience. It is amazing how many adult minds give evidence of lack of commitment to the laws of reason.

Speaking of logical (not chronological) priority, I believe the first step in any knowledge process must be *faith in reason*. It can be shown that faith is necessary in abstract mathematics, in formal logic, and in the physical and biological sciences just as truly as faith is necessary in the acceptance of Christianity. In his work on Existentialism, Kaufmann quotes Jaspers as saying that no one can understand his philosophy if he is not willing to "beat the other wing."[14] Jaspers means that in his writings, which Kaufmann describes as extended monologues, he is beating one wing, but if the mind of the reader is to soar, the reader must be willing to beat the other wing. By this Jaspers means to emphasize the volitional element in philosophical understanding.

[14]*Op. cit.*, p. 25.

CONCLUSION

We present then the following system of epistemology:
(1) Our elementary intuitive experiences are not mere sensations but dynamic situations. (2) Intuitive experiences lead to the acceptance of the outer world of things and persons. (3) Intuitive experiences lead to the acceptance of the laws of reason. (4) By the processes of faith, an integrated comprehension may be attained, the primary factors in which are (a) divine revelation, (b) reasonable knowledge of the ontological world, and (c) reasonable understanding of the laws of reason itself.

EPILOGUE

And now some student is heard to say in disappointment, "Is that all that philosophy can do for me?"

What did you expect?

"I expected a tool like a great wrench, or a lever with a fulcrum like Archimedes' *pou sto,* by which to move the world! I expected to be taught how to compel the minds of men, and turn them irresistibly to the truth."

Patience! You have good and useful tools. Philosophy, that is, true Christian philosophy, cannot compel. It can only help to clarify and remove some of the problems. Philosophy is not a substitute for the miracle of grace. It does not take the place of the convicting and regenerating work of the Holy Spirit of God. It is one of the instruments, in the hand of a born-again witness, which may be used by the Holy Spirit to bring about conviction and decision.

From your study of philosophy you should have gained three things: (1) a sympathetic understanding of some of the problems with which men who grope for the light are confronted; (2) an understanding of some of the answers to some of the problems; and (3) a broadening and deepening, and a systematization of your own grasp of God's truth.

"Having then a great High Priest who has passed through the heavens, [*kratomen tes 'omologias*] let us masterfully possess our profession" (Hebrews 4:14).

SUGGESTED ASSIGNMENTS

Instead of exact page references, or, worse yet, a book of fragments for outside reading assignments, the following suggestions are designed to induce the student to use the library with considerable initiative of his own. Of course, the richer the library collection the better, but the suggested work can be done with only a modest collection of the most commonly available authors and the most essential general reference works.

There are fifteen assignments, which, allowing for tests and holidays, facilitate the use of this textbook for a one semester course. The amount and the quality of the library work will vary with the maturity of the students. On the seminary level the students should be expected to plow deep, and cover broad fields. On the junior college level the work should probably occupy two semesters, the textbook material for each assignment being taken up first, then the corresponding library assignment the following week.

The textbook itself endeavors to be self-explanatory, but the student must be expected constantly to use the large dictionaries.

I. Introduction and Chapter I through page 19, which includes our viewpoint and introductory definitions.

As a first assignment the student should make the acquaintance of the chief general dictionaries and encyclopedias. Locate in your reference library, at least the *Encyclopaedia Britannica*, Baldwin's *Dictionary of Philosophy and Psychology*, Runes' *Dictionary of Philosophy*, and an *unabridged* recent edition of *Webster's Dictionary*. Bring to class a critical comparison of important definitions in the first assignment in this textbook with definitions found in these other reference works.

II. Pages 19 through 32, philosophy and other studies.

Browse through the books on "History of Philosophy" (Windelband is especially good for this purpose) and note some of the subjects such as physics, biology, politics, etc., which were discussed in ancient philosophy, though not now included in the philosophy department. An encyclopedia article on ancient Greek philosophy will help in preparing your report.

III. Pages 33 to 48, the categories.

Browse through the section of your library which has general works on philosophy or introductory textbooks. Find and compare other opinions on the definition of "time" and "space." To locate topics in such books use the indexes and the tables of contents. Write out your own ideas of the meanings of these terms.

IV. Pages 49 to 62, the categories, continued.

Look up Hume's discussion of causality. Check the specific references given in the text and read the contexts in Hume's own writings. Encyclopedia articles on "Hume" and on "Cause" will give you condensed material.

V. Pages 62 to 76, the categories, concluded, and materialism.

Investigate the view of "Pure Being" taught by Thomas Aquinas. Read the contexts of references given in the textbook. Try to grasp the concept of "being," which is not being in some category other than being. Try to defend Thomas' view against the view advanced in the text. If you cannot, state why.

VI. Pages 76 through 86, materialism, continued.

Check the references to Hobbes given in the text and examine the contexts. Read enough of *Leviathan* to gain a general impression and report your reaction.

VII. Pages 86 through 97, materialism, concluded.

Read some encyclopedia article on emergentism, or examine some book or books which discuss the topic. Prepare your own definition of what the term means to those who advance the theory of emergence. Carefully distinguish the emergence of values and forms from the emergence of substantive entities. Bring out, in your definition, the difference between the notion of something new from something old, and the notion of something from nothing.

VIII. Pages 98 to 111, idealism.

Check the contexts of the quotations in the textbook from Berkeley and/or Plato. Read enough of Plato to gain a clear impression. Prepare a summary and critique of what you cover.

IX. Pages 111 to 121, idealism, continued.

Select one of the idealists discussed in this part of the textbook, one whose chief writings are available in your library. Check the contexts of quotations given. Read additional material from this writer sufficient to gain a clear impression. Prepare a summary and critique of what you cover.

X. Pages 121 to 134, near idealisms, recapitulation, dualistic realism.

If available, read Chapter II (Kilpatrick, "Dewey's Views") and Chapter III (Breed, "Realism") in the forty-first yearbook of the N. S. S. E., Part I, *Philosophies of Education;* or read Chapter I (Wild, "Realism") and Chapter V (Geiger, "Dewey's Experimentalism") in the fifty-fourth yearbook, Part I, *Modern Philosophies and Education.* Both books are distributed by University of Chicago Press. If neither of these books is available, read and report on encyclopedia articles on Realism, Pragmatism and related subjects.

XI. Pages 134 to 146, dualistic realism, concluded, matter, mind.

Look up Kant's view of mind in relation to the material world. The chapter on Kant in Will Durant's *Story of Philosophy* is excellent, as is Robert Flint's treatment in his *Agnosticism.* Encyclopedia articles on Kant's philosophy will do.

Investigate the Biblical doctrine of *the soul* as a non-material substantive entity. Begin with articles in some accepted Bible Dictionary such as Davis' fourth edition, or some Bible Encyclopedia such as the "International Standard." Much material will be found in Hastings' B. D. and E. R. E. and in the Schaff-Herzog *Encyclopaedia of Religious Knowledge.* Define your thoughts on the interaction of soul and body.

XII. Pages 147 through 160, ontological causality.

Read and report on dictionary and encyclopedia articles on "Cause" or "Causality." See for example F. R. Tennant's article in Hastings E. R. E., Vol. III.

XIII. Pages 162 to 175, between ontology and epistemology, a priori views.

Investigate your available reference works until you are sure you can distinguish between *a priori* reasoning and inductive reasoning. Report on your findings and support your conclusions.

XIV. Pages 175 to 184, common ground, constructive suggestions.

Check the references to Calvin's Institutes in their contexts. Read enough in the Institutes to make sure you have a fair idea of Calvin's methods of reasoning. Report your findings.

XV. Pages 184 to 200, constructive suggestions, concluded, the laws of reason, conclusion, epilogue.

Spend the major part of your outside reading time for this last assignment, not in reading, but in meditating on the laws of reason, and on what you may have gained from your study of philosophy thus far. Write a summary of your conclusions.

SELECTED BIBLIOGRAPHY

The purpose of this bibliography is to provide a minimum list of reference works which ought to be available to the student in the introductory course presented in this textbook. Not at all comprehensive, the list does not even include all the works referred to in the text. Strictly a minimum list, it is suggested that the students should have at least these works available; some for reference, some for browsing, and some for extensive reading. If some of these titles are not available the teacher and the librarian may be able to secure equivalent works.

General Reference Works

For remarkably concise definitions and summaries of philosophical systems:

Webster's Dictionary of the English Language. Second edition. Unabridged. Springfield, Mass.: G. and C. Merriam, 1952.

For the widest scholarly and historical reference:
Encyclopaedia Britannica. University of Chicago Press.

For readable, accurate, scholarly reference:
The World Book Encyclopaedia. 20 vols. Field Enterprises Educational Corporation.

Dictionaries of Philosophy

BALDWIN, J. MARK. (ed.) *Dictionary of Philosophy and Psychology.* 3 vols. New York: Peter Smith, corrected edition, 1925.

RUNES, DAGOBERT D. (ed.) *Dictionary of Philosophy.* New York: Philosophical Library, 1944 or 1945.

Journals

The library should provide the files of some general philosophical journal or journals such as:

SCHNEIDER, HERBERT W., and RANDALL, JOHN H., JR. (eds.) *The Journal of Philosophy.* Published fortnightly. 713 Philosophy Hall, Columbia University, New York 27, N. Y. (Complete files for the past twenty years, at least, should be available for reference.)

Selected Bibliography

Encyclopedias of Religion

HARRISON, EVERETT F. (ed.) *Baker's Dictionary of Theology.* Grand Rapids: Baker Book House, 1959.

HASTINGS, JAMES. (ed.) *Encyclopaedia of Religion and Ethics.* 13 vols., including index. New York: Scribners, 1908.

JACKSON, SAMUEL MACAULEY. (ed.) *The New Schaff-Herzog Encyclopaedia of Religious Knowledge.* 13 vols., including index. New York: Funk and Wagnalls, 1908. Recent reprint, Grand Rapids: Baker Book House.

LOETSCHER, LEFFERTS A. (ed.) *Twentieth Century Encyclopaedia of Religious Knowledge.* (An extension of *The New Schaff-Herzog Encyclopaedia of Religious knowledge.*) 2 vols. Grand Rapids: Baker Book House, 1955.

Histories of Philosophy

DURANT, WILL. *The Story of Philosophy.* New York: Simon and Schuster, 1928.

WEBER, ALFRED, and THILLY, FRANK. (tr.) *History of Philosophy,* with Ralph Barton Perry's *Philosophy Since 1860.* New York: Scribners, 1925.

WINDELBAND, W., and TUFTS, JAMES H. (tr.) *History of Philosophy.* Second edition. New York: Macmillan, 1938.

Religious Systems

Conservative systems of Christian thought:

CALVIN, JOHN. *Institutes of the Christian Religion.* Last revision by Calvin, 1559. Available in several editions. Recent reprint, Grand Rapids: Eerdmans.

CLARK, GORDON H. *A Christian Philosophy of Education.* Grand Rapids: Eerdmans, 1946.

————. *A Christian View of Men and Things.* Grand Rapids: Eerdmans, 1952.

FLINT, ROBERT. *Theism.* New York: Scribner's, 1893.

————. *Anti-Theistic Theories.* New York: William Blackwood and Sons, 1894.

————. *Agnosticism.* New York: Scribner's, 1903.

HODGE, CHARLES. *Systematic Theology.* 3 vols. New York: Scribner's, 1871. Current reprint by Eerdmans.

ORR, JAMES. *The Christian View of God and the World.* New York: Scribner's, 1897.

YOUNG, WARREN C. *A Christian Approach to Philosophy.* Grand Rapids: Baker Book House, 1954.

Liberal systems:

BRIGHTMAN, EDGAR SHEFFIELD. *A Philosophy of Religion.* New York: Prentice Hall, 1945.

Selected Bibliography

KILLEN, R. ALLEN. *The Ontological Theology of Paul Tillich.* Holland: Kampen, 1956.

TENNANT, F. R. *Philosophical Theology.* 2 vols. New York: Cambridge University Press, 1928.

TILLICH, PAUL. *Systematic Theology.* 2 vols., vol. 3 to appear later. Chicago: University of Chicago Press.

General Works on Logic

COPI, IRVING M. *Introduction to Logic.* New York: Macmillan, 1954. (Includes an introduction to symbolic logic.)

JEVONS, W. STANLEY. *Elementary Lessons in Logic.* New York: Macmillan, 1914. (A classic, easy to read.)

ROBINSON, DANIEL SOMMER. *Principles of Reasoning.* Third edition. New York: Appleton-Century, 1947. (Adds the "Law of Sufficient Reason.")

Classics, Historical and Recent Types of Philosophy

AYER, A. J. (ed.) *Logical Positivism.* Glencoe, Illinois: The Free Press, 1959.

BARRETT, BAKEWELL, HOCKING, CUNNINGHAM, URBAN, LEIGHTON, BRIGHTMAN, BOODIN, TSANOFF, HENDEL, HOERNLE. *Contemporary Idealism in America.* New York: Macmillan, 1932.

BERTOCCI, PETER ANTHONY. *The Empirical Argument for God in Late British Thought.* Cambridge: Harvard University Press, 1938.

BRIDGMAN, P. W. *The Logic of Modern Physics.* New York: Macmillan, 1927. Reprint 1946.

BURTT, E. A. (ed.) *English Philosophers from Bacon to Mill.* New York: Random House, Modern Library, 1939.

BUSWELL, J. O. JR. *Philosophies of F. R. Tennant and John Dewey.* New York: Philosophical Library, 1950.

BUTLER, JOSEPH. *The Analogy of Religion to the Constitution and Course of Nature.* First published in 1736. Available in many editions.

DEWEY, JOHN. *The Quest for Certainty.* New York: George Allen and Unwin, 1930.

—————. *Art as Experience.* New York: Milton Balch and Co., 1934.

—————. *Logic – the Theory of Inquiry.* New York: Henry Holt and Co., 1938.

DRAKE, LOVEJOY, PRATT, ROGERS, SANTAYANA, SELLARS, STRONG. *Essays in Critical Realism.* New York: Macmillan, 1920.

FEUERBACH, LUDWIG. *The Essence of Christianity.* George Eliot (tr.) New York: Harpers, reprint 1957. (Introduction by Karl Barth, Foreword by Richard Niebuhr.)

HENRY, NELSON B. (ed.) *Philosophies of Education.* Forty-first Yearbook, National Society for the Study of Education. Chicago: University of Chicago Press, 1942.

207

—————. *Modern Philosophies and Education.* Fifty-fourth Yearbook, National Society for the Study of Education. Chicago: University of Chicago Press, 1956.

HOBBES, THOMAS. *Leviathan.* Available in several editions. No. 691 of Everyman's Library.

HOLT, MARVIN, MONTAGUE, PERRY, PITKIN, SPAULDING. *The New Realism.* New York: Macmillan, 1912.

HOYLE, FRED. *The Nature of the Universe.* New York: Harpers, 1950.

—————. *Frontiers of Astronomy.* New York: Mentor, Harpers, 1957.

HUME, DAVID. *Selections.* Charles W. Hendel (ed.) New York: Scribner's, 1927.

JOWETT, B. (ed.) *The Dialogues of Plato.* 2 vols. New York: Random House, 1937.

KANT, IMMANUEL. *Selections.* T. M. Greene (ed.) New York: Scribner's, 1929. (Over 500 pages of Kant's most important writings with a valuable introduction.)

KNUDSON, ALBERT C. *The Philosophy of Personalism.* Boston: Boston University Press, 1949.

KRIKORIAN, Y. H. (ed.) *Naturalism and the Human Spirit.* New York: Columbia University Press, 1945.

LEIBNIZ, GOTTFRIED WILHELM. *Selections.* Philip P. Wiener (ed.) New York: Scribner's, 1951.

MCKEON, RICHARD. (ed.) *The Basic Works of Aristotle.* New York: Random House, 1941.

MARX, KARL. *Capital — A Critique of Political Economy.* Fredrick Engels (ed.) New York: Random House, Modern Library, 1906. (Available in several editions.)

NEWTON, ISAAC. *Principia Mathematica.* Originally published in Latin, 1713. Florian Cajori (ed.) Berkeley: University of California Press, 1946.

ORR, JOHN. *English Deism — Its Roots and Its Fruits.* Grand Rapids: Eerdmans, 1934.

PEGIS, ANTON C. (ed.) *Basic Writings of St. Thomas Aquinas.* 2 vols. New York: Random House, 1945.

ROBINSON, DANIEL SOMMER. *Crucial Issues in Philosophy.* New York: Christopher Press, 1955.

RUNES, DAGOBERT. (ed.) *Twentieth Century Philosophies.* New York: Philosophical Library, 1943.

SPIER, J. M. *Christianity and Existentialism.* David Hugh Freeman (tr.) Presbyterian and Reformed Publishing Co., n. d.

STACE, W. T. *The Philosophy of Hegel.* First edition, 1923. Dover Press, reprint, 1955.

INDEX

Absolute Idealism, 116
Absolute Mind, 113, 125
Abstraction, 41
Aesthetics, 20, 21, 24, 164
 and Logic, 23
 and Philosophy, 24
 and Presuppositions, 25
 and Psychology, 28
"Amazing Grace," 156
Angels and Spirits, Hobbes' View, 78
Anselm of Canterbury, 110
A Priori Theories, 168-177, 190
 Theistic, 170 ff.
 Rationalistic, 172 ff.
Arbitrary Will, 190 ff.
Areopagus, 115
Aristotle, 29, 31, 34, 35, 46, 48
 on Cause, 57
 on Time, 44 ff.
Atheism, Dogmatic, 81 f.
Atheists and Anti-Theists, 172
Athenian Philosophical Association, 115
Atomistic Psychology, 183
Atomists, 71 f.
Atoms, Free Will, 74
Atonement, 10
Augustine, 46, 101
Axiology, 26, 98
Ayer, A. J., 29

Bakewell, 125
Barrett, 125
Barth, Karl, 121, 192
Behaviorism, 17
Being, Category of, 63
 Definition of, 15
 and Existence, 64
 and Reality, 65
 Theory of, 68
Bergson, 123
Berkeley, George, 103, 106, 146, 149, 180
 on Economics, 104
 on Knowledge of God, 106
 on Knowledge of Other Persons, 106
 and Locke, 104
 Missionary Interest, 103
Bertocci, Peter, 112, 114
Bible, as Authority, 9
 and Materialism, 71
 Psychological Terms, 142 f.
Biology, 20, 29

Body and Mind, 156, 157, 159
 and Soul, 140 f.
Boodin, 125
Bowne, Borden Parker, 111 ff.
Brain and Mind, 141
"Brain Track" Psychology, 142
Breed, Frederick, 130
Bridgman, 38
Brightman, 112, 125
Broad, C. D., 127
Brute Facts, 155 f.
Buber, Martin, 21
Burtt, Edwin A., 103
Butler, Joseph, 139

Cabanis, 80
Cajori, Florian, 60
Calvin, John, and Presuppositionalism, 176 f.
Carnap, Rudolph, 29, 122
Categories, 33-66
 Agreement in, 35
 Being, 63
 Causation, 54
 Clarity of, 34, 66
 as Class Predicates, 34
 Conscious States, 62
 Consistency in, 35
 Comprehensiveness of, 34
 and Discourse, 35 f.
 and Epistemology, 35
 of Naturalism, 51
 Number, 52
 and Ontology, 35
 Quantity, 52
 Space, 34-41
 Time, 41-45
 Value, 63
Causality, 147 ff.
Causation, Category of, 54-61
 Complexity of, 57 f.
 Creditable or Chargeable, 58
 Definition of, 56
 and Effect, 55
 Effective Power, 57
 and Implication, 56, 145
 Interaction, 156
 Mechanical, 56, 57, 59, 147
 Psychological, 149
 and Sequence, 56
 Theistic View, 61
 Universality, 58, 61 f., 149
Certainty, 28

209

Certitude, 28
Chemistry, 20
Childhood Faith, 197f.
"Christian Science," 197
Chronos and Time, 44
Cicero, 139
Classification of Sciences, 19f.
"Closed System," 157
Cohen, 164
Coherence, 192
"Common Ground," 175
"Common Sense" Philosophy, 131
Complex Unity, 17
Comte, Auguste, 122
Condorcet, 80
Consciousness, 18
  and Materialism, 79, 96
Conscious States, Category of, 62
Conservation of Energy, 70
  of Matter, 70
Consistency, 192
Contradictories, Law of, 21, 185, 187
Convictions, 7
Correspondence, 192
Cosmic Process, Beginning of, 46
Cosmogony, 132
Cosmological Argument, 176
Cosmology, 131
Cosmonomic Idea, Philosophy of, 177
Creation, 8, 61, 76, 91, 107
Criteria of Laws of Reason, 189
Critical Realism, 130
Cullmann, Oscar, on Time in New
  Testament, 47

D'Alembert, 80
Definitions, 15
Degrees of Reality, 100, 101, 111
Deism, 79
Democritus, 71-75
Dennes, William R., 51
Descartes, 36, 37, 111, 139, 155, 157
Determinism, 149
Dewey, John, 21, 33, 37, 83, 84, 88,
  89, 122, 128, 133, 134, 169, 189f.,
  194
  Goals, 129
  and Materialism, 124
  Metaphysics, 123, 128
Dialectical Materialism, 89
Dialectics, 83, 191f.
Dictatorship of Proletariat, 86
Diderot, 80
Dilettante Methods, 7
Dimensionalism, 21
Dimensions, Figurative and Literal, 39
Discourse, Categories of, 35
Divergent Views, 31

Dooyeweerd, Herman, 177
Drake, Durant, 130, 164
Dualism, in Epistemology, 178
  Eternal Metaphysical, 131
  Ethical, 131
  Objections to, 17
Dualistic Idealism, 99
Dualistic Realism, 8, 19, 27, 51, 126
  130, 160, 164, 197
Duration, 37
  Relative, 41f.
Dynamic Situations, 180-184

Economics, 165f.
Eddington, 37, 135
Edel, Abraham, 68f.
Edwards, Jonathan, 133, 155
Effect and Cause, 55
Einstein, 29
Elementary Intuitive Experience,
  179f., 182, 197
Emergentism, 61, 94
Emergentistic Materialism, 88f., 92
Empirical Arguments of Jesus, 170
Empirical Evidence in Bible, 170
Empiricism, History of, 169
  and Revelation, 169
Engels, 83f.
Ens Perfectissimum, 102
Ens Realissimum, 102
Entities, Substantive, 36
Epicurus, Epicureans, 72, 74, 115
Epilogue, 200
Epiphenomenalism, 127, 158f.
Epistemology, 8, 16f., 20, 31, 130,
  162-198
  Dualism, 178
  and Idealism, 98
  and Logic, 22
  and Mathematics, 30
  and Metaphysics, 178
  and Ontology, 197
  and Psychology, 28
  Systems of, 199
"Eternal Sin," 152
Ethics, 9, 20, 21, 25, 73, 130, 164
  and Axiology, 26
  Dualistic, 131
  and Logic, 23
  Materialistic, 81
  and Philosophy, 25
  and Psychology, 28
Excluded Middle, Law of, 188
Existence, 15
  Ambiguity of, 64
Existentialism, 21, 33, 65
Experience and Duration, 41
Experimentalism, 17, 37, 51, 124

210

Extended Things; *see Res Extensa*
Extension, 37
    Experience of, 38
    and Measurement, 38 f.
Evangelism, Tactics, 169, 171
"Evidences," 171
Evolution, 29

Factual Revelation, 174
Faith, of a Child, 197 f.
    Objective and Subjective, 195
    a Principle of Reason, 194 f., 196,
        198
    and Understanding, 195
Feuerbach, 27, 83
Finitude of God, Alleged, 114
Flint, Robert, 75 f., 80, 189
Franciscan, on Thomas Aquinas, 112
Free Will, Nature of, 150-154
Fritz, Charles A., Jr., 168
Fullerton, George Stuart, 126, 133,
    151
Functionalism, 27

Gassendi, 76 f., 79
Geometry, Euclidean, 23
Gestalt Psychology, 24, 179, 181-184,
    196, 198
God, Alleged Finitude, 114
    Cause, 154
    Character and Will, 25, 154, 155,
        165, 193 f.
    Grace of, 23
    Holiness of, 165
    and Materialism, 97
    Miracles of, 200
    not in any Genus?, 64 f.
Green, T. H., 116, 123
Grounds of Belief, Not Tactics, 171 f.

Hackett, Stuart C., 59, 174
Hedonism, 73
Helvetius, 80
Hegel, 83 f.
    Logic of, 83
Heim, Karl, 21
Heisenberg Principle, 29, 147
Helium and Hydrogen, 29, 92
Hendel, 125
Hepp, 176
Hobbes, Thomas, Materialism of, 76-
    80, 90
    and Charles II, 79
    and Incomprehensibility of God, 79
Hocking, 112, 125
Hodge, Charles, 96, 129, 155, 158,
    189
    on Causality, 55
    on Edwards and Shedd, 133

Hoernle, 125
Holbach, P. H. D. von, 80
Holiness of God, 165
Holt, 130
Holy Spirit and Philosophy, 200
Hook, Sidney, 61, 88
Hormic Psychology, 158
Horne, Herman H., 113, 116
Hoyle, Fred, and Emergentism, 90-95
Hume, David, 122, 144, 145, 149,
    158, 180
    on Causality, 55
    on Ego, 143 f.
Husserl, Edmund, 121
Hydrogen and Helium, 29, 92

Idealism, 17, 51, 98-125, 130
    Absolute, 116
    of Berkeley, 103-107
    Definition of, 98
    Dualistic, 99
    Epistemological, 98
    of Leibnitz, 120 f.
    Metaphysical, 99
    Monistic, 99
    Personalistic, 110-116
    and Phenomenology, 122
    of Plato, 107-111
    of Urban, 116-120
    Survey, 125
Ideas, Innate, 190
Identity, Law of, 187
Immortality, 73
Implication and Causality, 145
Implicative System; *see* Law of
    Sufficient Reason
Indefinable, 41
Indeterminacy, 29, 147-149
Inductive Arguments, Value of, 173
Inductive Reasoning, 168 f.
Infinity, Not a "Whole," 31, 54
    Paradox of, 54
Innate Ideas, 190
Instants, Not Parts of Time, 48
Instrumentalism, 124
Integration, 18 f.
Interaction, 133, 156 f., 159
Intuitive Experience, Elementary,
    179 f., 182, 197
Irrational, 23
Iverach, James, 130, 163, 178 f.

James, William, 180
Jaspers, 198
Jesus Christ, Crucifixion, 10
    Empirical Arguments of, 170
    Historical, 174
Johnson, Elias H., 129

Kairos and Time, 44
Kant, Immanuel, 35, 56, 64, 111, 129, 174, 180
Kaufmann, 198
Kierkegaard, 173, 192
Knowledge, Intuitive, 179
    Steps, 180
Knudson, 111-113
Kroeber, A. L., 30

Laboratory Sciences and Psychology, 28
Lalande, 80
Lamettrie, 80
Lange, F. A., 72, 74-76, 78-80
Laplace, 60
Law of Sufficient Reason, 23, 58, 59
    of Contradictories, 185, 192
    of Excluded Middle, 188
    of Identity, 187
Laws of Reason, 189 f.
    Criteria of, 189
    Source of, 193 f.
    Learning, 166 f.
Leibnitz, 23, 58, 119 f., 127, 149, 157
Leighton, 125
Levi, A. W., 123
Locke, John, 55, 73, 104, 120, 158, 180
Lodge, Ruppert C., 103
Logic, 20
    and Aesthetics, 23
    and Appropriateness, 23 f.
    and Epistemology, 22
    and Ethics, 23
    of Hegel, 83
    Laws of, 9
    and Mathematics, 22, 30
    and Metaphysics, 22
    Multi-valued, 188
    and Psychology, 22, 28
    Standards of, 21
    Two-valued, 188
Logical Positivism, 29, 122 f.
Lovejoy, 130
Lucretius, 72, 74, 75

Marcus Aurelius, 75
Marechal, 80
Marvin, 130
Marx, Karl, 26, 83, 84
    Economic Fallacies, 87
Materialism, 17, 37, 69-97, 126, 132
    and Atheism, 82
    and Consciousness, 96
    Definition of, 69 ff.
    Dialectic, 85 f.
    Emergentistic, 88

and Ethics, 81
    French, 80
    and French Revolution, 82
    and God, 97
    Historical Systems, 95
    Implicit, 70
    Materialistic Dialectic, 85 f.
    Material Universe, Eternal?, 62
Mathematics, 20, 29
    and Epistemology, 30
    and Logic, 22, 30
    and Metaphysics, 30
    and Philosophy, 29
Matter, and Mind, 96 f.
    Nature of, 134, 138 f.
McCosh, James, 131
McDougall, William, 158
McGill, V. J., 126, 128
Measurement, and Extension, 38 f.
    Experience of, 38
Mechanism and Cause, 59, 60, 147-149
Mental Images, 63
Metaphysical Idealism, 99
Metaphysics, 8, 16, 20, 163
    and Epistemology, 178
    and Logic, 22
    and Mathematics, 30
    and Psychology, 27
Mill, John Stuart, 114
Mind, Absolute, 113, 125
    and Body, 89, 156, 157, 159
    and Brain, 141 f.
    Nature of, 139
    Universal, 113, 116, 123
Miracle of Grace, 200
Monism, 18
Monistic Idealism, 99
Montague, 130
Moses, 174
Multi-valued Logic, 188

Nagel, 88
Naigeon, 80
Napoleon, 60
Naturalism, 18, 51, 88
"Natural Philosophy," 29
Nature, Order of, 184
Near-Idealism, 120
Neo-Hegelianism, 116
New Realism, 130
Newton, Sir Isaac, 60
Nietzsche, 196 f.
Nominalism, 102
Non-Rational, 23
Normative Science, 21
Number, Category of, 52
    Definition, 53

Distinction from Quantity, 53
Numerical Identity, 157
Numerical Otherness, 157

Objective Reality, 197
Occult, 160
Omnipotence Denied, 114 f.
Ontological Argument, 110
Ontology, 17, 68, 130, 163
    Definition of, 15
    and Epistemology, 197
Order of Nature, 184
Order of Valid Thought, 185
Original Sin, 9, 11
Orr, James, 80
Orr, John, 79
Otherness, Numerical, 157

Palmer, 125
Pantheism and Personalism, 112, 113
Paradox, 191 f.
    of Infinity, 54
    of Space, 47
    of Time, 47
Parallelism, 126, 133, 151
Peirce, C. S., 177
Perception, Memory, Imagination, 63
Perry, Ralph Barton, 130
Personal Causation, 62, 111-116
    and Pantheism, 112 f.
Phenomenology, 121 f.
    and Realism, 122
Philosophical Jungles, 114 f.
Philosophy, Cannot Compel, 200
    Definition of, 15
    and Aesthetics, 24
    and Ethics, 25
    and Mathematics, 29
    and Social Sciences, 26
Physics, 20, 29, 61
Pitkin, 130
Plato, 72, 102
    Alcibiades, 140 f.
    Idealism, 107-111
Pluralism, 18 f.
Plurality and Unity, 16, 19
Point of View of This Book, 7
Points, Not Parts of Lines, 48
Pragmatism, 37, 124
Pratt, 130
Predication, 33
Presuppositionalism, 175-177
    and Aesthetics, 25
    Calvin's View, 176 f.
Presuppositions, 8, 11
"Process" Philosophy, 123
Proletarian Revolution, 86
Psychological Causation, 149

Psychology, 20, 27
    and Aesthetics, 28
    and Epistemology, 28
    and Ethics, 28
    Experimental, 28
    and Laboratory Science, 28
    and Logic, 22, 28
    and Metaphysics, 27
    and Mind, 27
    and Psyche, 27
    and Social Sciences, 28
Pythagoras, 29

Qualities, Additive, 49
    Conflicting Definitions, 50 f.
    Definitive, 49
    Numerous Kinds, 52
    Primary and Secondary, 49, 163
    Relational, 163 f.
    Sensory, 50
    Tertiary, 52
    Valuational, 52
Quality, Category of, 49
Quantity, Category of, 52
Quantum Theory, 147

Randall, John Herman, 33
"Rational Empiricism," 59
Rationalism, 58
Rationalistic A Priori, 173 f.
Realism, 98, 136 f.
    Aesthetic, 132 f.
    of Ideas, 133
    Medieval and Modern, 102
    and Phenomenology, 122
Realistic Dualism; see Dualistic
    Realism
Reality, 33
    and Being, 65
    Degrees of, 100 f., 111
    and Value, 100
Reason, Laws of; see Laws of Reason
Reason and Faith, 196
Reason, the Cause of Being?, 23
Reck, Andrew J., 123
Reference Works, Use of, 31
Reflex Arc Concept, 123
Reichenbach, Hans, 122
Reid, Thomas, 130
Representative Principle, 10 f.
Res Cogitans, 27, 36 f., 69, 90, 100,
    142, 178, 199
Res Extensa, 27, 69, 100, 139, 178
Revelation and Empiricism, 169
Revolution, Proletarian, 86
Rhetoric, Aristotle's, 19
Ritschl, Albrecht, 21
Robinson, Daniel Sommer, 23, 58 f.,
    125, 139

Rogers, 130
Royce, Josiah, 23, 116, 125
Russell, Bertrand, 46, 64, 72

Santayana, George, 46, 127, 130, 158
Saul of Tarsus, Conversion of, 151 f.
Schilpp, Paul Arthur, 29
Scholar's Burden, 31
Scientific Method, 12, 21, 173
Second Law of Thermodynamics, 29
Secondary Qualities, 163
"Self Evident" Principles, 190
Sellars, 130
Sensations, 181 f.
Shedd, William G. T., 133
Sheldon, 88
Social Sciences, 20
    and Philosophy, 26
    and Psychology, 28
Social Values, 165
Sociology, 165
Socrates, 71
Solipsism, 107
Soul, 27
    and Body, 140 f.
    Hobbes' View, 77
    Materialistic View, 69
Space, 34-47
    Assumptions, 37
    Boundaries, 40
    Container, 40
    Definition of, 40 f.
    Paradoxes, 47
Spaulding, 130
Spirit, the Only Substance?, 105
Spontaneity, 149 f.
Square of Opposition, 186 f.
Stace, W. T., 116
Steps in Knowledge, 180
Stoicism, 75, 115
    Determinism, 76
    Materialism, 75 f.
Strong, Augustus Hopkins, 129 f.
Subjective Consciousness, 37
Substantive Entity, 36
Sufficient Reason, Law of, 23, 58 f.
System, Definition of, 173 f.

Tactics, in Evangelism, 169 f.
    not Grounds of Belief, 171 f.
Teleological Argument, 176
Teleology, Inorganic, 94
Tennant, F. R., 37, 94, 156, 158, 169,
    180, 183, 197
    on Causality, 57
    Metaphysics of, 124
Tertiary Qualities, 164
Theism, 8
    and Causality, 61
Theory of Knowledge, 16

Thermodynamics, Second Law of, 29
Thinking Things; see Res Cogitans
Thomas Aquinas, 64, 102
Time, Category of, 34, 37, 41-45
    Aristotle's View, 44 ff.
    and Chronos, 44
    not a Container, 43
    Definition of, 47
    and Duration, 41
    Figurative and Literal, 42
    not a Flowing Substance, 43
    and Kairos, 44
    not Limited, 44
    and Number, 45
    Paradoxes of, 47
Tools, Good and Useful, 200
Trichotomy, 142 f.
Trigger Action, 158
Tsanoff, 125
Two-valued Logic, 188
Tyndale, 96

"Unaskable" Questions, 123
Understanding and Faith, 195
Unified Complexity, 17
Unit, Definition of, 53
Unity and Plurality, 16, 19
Universal Causality, 61 f., 149
Universal Mind, 113, 116, 123
Universals, 102 f.
Urban, Wilbur Marshall, Idealism of,
    116-120, 125
    on Symbolic Language, 119 f.

Valid Thought, Order of, 185
Value, 63, 164
    Category of, 63
    and Reality, 110
    Social, 165
    Varieties of, 63
Van Til, Cornelius, 176
Vienna Circle, 122
Vincent of Lerins, 132
Vocabulary, New, 31

Watson, J. B., 17
"Wavicles," 38
Wells, H. G., 114
Whitehead, 123
Wholeness, 19
Wild, John, 130
Windelband, 80
Wisdom, Bipolar, 15
Witsidee, Philosophy of, 177
Wittgenstein, Ludwig, 122

Xenophon, 72

Young, Warren C., 116, 122, 169

Zeno, 48, 75